CHOOSING HEAVEN

—

MORE THAN SAYING A PRAYER

A SOUL SEARCHING ADVENTURE
NATHAN RENE COLAW

THANKS

Thank you, Carolyn Hackney, Mary Maness, Shari Sauer, and Sara Colaw for your help with the editing.

Thanks to Roger Skelly's Sunday School class for helping me with this project. They did not know they were helping, but Sunday after Sunday, Sara and I would comment that the lesson and the comments from the class were along the same line that I had been writing during the previous week. It was almost as if they had access to my computer and knew what I was writing, and they wanted to help. I considered that confirmation.

My pastor and little brother Joe also helped me in this process. His sermons often confirmed what I was writing. With his permission, I used some of his sermon materials.

At times when I wanted to know how others were thinking about a subject, I would post a paragraph or so from my writings on Facebook and ask for feedback. Many Facebook friends gave me feedback. Thanks to all of you!

The Cover

You may not have even noticed the cover picture. I chose it purposefully. Life has some mountains to climb and some clouds that darken our days.

Do not focus on the clouds and the mountains. Focus on the light just over the mountains and beyond the clouds. That is heaven.

The dark clouds and the mountains cannot keep you from reaching the light – heaven, if you really want to get there.

Keep your eyes on the light and do not let anything stop you from reaching it. You can move out of the darkness into the light. Inside this book are clear instructions on how to do it.

Table of Contents

INTRODUCTION

Billy Graham said, **"Man cannot solve his problems without Jesus Christ."**

Man has a big problem. Unless he has a Savior – someone to rescue him from his sinful condition, he has no hope. He will live a sinful life and die a sinner on the way to hell. Some will say that statement is too harsh; can you say it with less sting? The answer is, probably. Maybe that is one of our problems now. We have down played the consequences of living without God and living in sin. We have watered down the consequences of sin, so people are not offended.

This book is straight talk about going or not going to heaven; so fasten your seat belt.

This book is not just about going to heaven; it is also about living a better, more satisfying, rewarding, and peaceful life here on this earth. A hymn tells about moving from the darkness of this world to the light of Christ.

JESUS I COME

Out of my bondage, sorrow, and night,
Jesus, I come, Jesus, I come;
Into Thy freedom, gladness, and light,
Jesus, I come to Thee;
Out of my sickness, into Thy health,
Out of my want and into Thy wealth,
Out of my sin and into Thyself,
Jesus, I come to Thee.

Out of my shameful failure and loss,
Jesus, I come, Jesus, I come;
Into the glorious gain of Thy cross,
Jesus, I come to Thee.
Out of earth's sorrows into Thy balm,

Out of life's storms and into Thy calm,
Out of distress to jubilant psalm,
Jesus, I come to Thee.

Out of unrest and arrogant pride,
Jesus, I come, Jesus, I come;
Into Thy blessèd will to abide,
Jesus, I come to Thee.
Out of myself to dwell in Thy love,
Out of despair into raptures above,
Upward for aye on wings like a dove,
Jesus, I come to Thee.

Out of the fear and dread of the tomb,
Jesus, I come, Jesus, I come;
Into the joy and light of Thy throne,
Jesus, I come to Thee.
Out of the depths of ruin untold,
Into the peace of Thy sheltering fold,
Ever Thy glorious face to behold,
Jesus, I come to Thee.

William T. Sleeper,
Gospel Hymns No. 5, 1887

THIS BOOK IS NOT…
- A "make me feel good" book - entertainment
- Another book trying to explain hard to understand biblical passages
- Another writer's speculation about what heaven is like

THIS BOOK IS ABOUT…
- Challenging you to become a better and happier person
- Experiencing a rewarding and fulfilling life here on this earth

- Experiencing a perfect life in heaven forever, after you leave this earth

This is one adventure that truly can make your life awesome. This book is about moving from darkness to light.

Moving from not knowing to knowing

Know what the Bible says. Some people do not know how to live so they can experience true satisfaction in life. Some people do not know what they need to do to be sure they will go to heaven. Some believe everyone is going to heaven. The Bible says not everyone will go to heaven. In fact, it says most will not. Surprised? You cannot plead ignorance at the pearly gates. "Sorry God, I did not know" will not fly. It is your responsibility to know what the Bible says. This book is full of scripture to help you know how to live a great life here on this earth and end up in heaven for eternity.

Moving from not doing to doing

One can know what to do and never do it. Do not confuse this with working your way to heaven. You cannot just decide to be a Christian; you have to become a Christian. The Bible says *"...all must repent of their sins and turn to God – and prove they have changed by the good things they do."* Acts 26:20 (NLT) If you are a true follower, your behavior – deeds – will reveal that. This book gives you a 1-2-3 – this is how you do it, formula to help you live a life that is pleasing and acceptable to God – it is called **THE PADD**. If you will use **THE PADD**, you can experience a great life here, and go to heaven.

Moving from this earth to heaven

It is the transition – the transformation from an imperfect earthly body to a perfect heavenly body.

Jesus said:

Matthew 13:41-43 (NIV)

The Son of Man (Jesus) will send out his angels, and they will weed out of his kingdom everything that causes sin and all who do evil. They will throw them into the fiery furnace, (hell) where there will be weeping and gnashing of teeth. Then the righteous will shine like the sun in the kingdom of their Father (heaven). He, who has ears, let him hear.

Do you want to experience a great life while here on this earth? You can!

Do you want to go to heaven? You can!

The goal of this book is to help you find yourself spiritually and help you know for sure you are ready for heaven and make you better equipped to help someone else prepare for heaven. It is my opinion based on 35+ years of pastoring and counseling that many people who think they are ready for heaven are not and they don't even know it.

This book can be used as a personal study book, possibly for one's personal devotional time. It can be used in a small group setting, allowing individuals to discuss and learn from each other and grow together.

In many books, you will find questions at the end of each chapter or at the end of the book to generate thought and cause the reader to become mentally engaged in the subject. For small groups the purpose of the questions is to create discussion.

You may like it that way. I prefer to talk about issues along the way while they are fresh in my thinking; rather than fill my mind with too much stuff, then try to sort it out at the end.

It is my opinion that the purpose of the questions should be to engage a person in the study as it progresses; not a test of the memory to see how much one can recall at the end of the chapter or book.

To enhance the purpose of this book, there are questions or instructions **("time outs")** scattered throughout each chapter to encourage you to stop, think, and relate.

In small groups, the questions can create general discussion about the world, our nation, the church as a whole or your specific church. These **"time-outs"** are great opportunities to make a life-changing decision and say, "This is talking about me; I need to do something about my life and the way I am living".

➢ *You will recognize the questions or instructions (timeouts) because they will appear in this format. They are "take action – do something" indicators.*

Some writers will make a great point and follow it up with just a scripture reference. The reader may not take time to pick up a Bible and look up the scripture, so he misses what God has to say. The strength, the best support for the point, is what God has to say. A friend taught me this valuable lesson. I would make a statement, and he would reply with, "And what scripture do you use to support that thought?" What God has to say about anything is more important than what all the writers together have to say. Considering that, you have the scripture written out right there for you almost all of the time.

The following scriptures are the basis for this book.

John 3:3 (TLB) Jesus said, "With all the earnestness I possess I tell you this: Unless you are born again, you can never get into the Kingdom of God."

Matthew 7:21-23 (TLB) 21 "Not all who sound religious are really godly people. They may refer to me as 'Lord,' but still won't get to heaven. For the decisive question is whether they

obey my Father in heaven.
22 At the Judgment many will tell me, 'Lord, Lord, we told others about you and used your name to cast out demons and to do many other great miracles.'
23 But I will reply, 'You have never been mine. Go away, for your deeds are evil.'

The Battle

Ephesians 6:12 (TLB) [12] *For we are not fighting against people made of flesh and blood, but against persons without bodies – the evil rulers of the unseen world, those mighty satanic beings and great evil princes of darkness who rule this world; and against huge numbers of wicked spirits in the spirit world.*

The Sentence

John 3:19-21 (TLB) 19 Their sentence is based on this fact: that the Light from heaven came into the world, but they loved the darkness more than the Light, for their deeds were evil.
20 They hated the heavenly Light because they wanted to sin in the darkness. They stayed away from that Light for fear their sins would be exposed and they would be punished.
21 But those doing right come gladly to the Light to let everyone see that they are doing what God wants them to."

The Hope

John 3:16-17 (TLB) [16]*For God loved the world so much that he gave his only Son so that anyone who believes in him shall not perish but have eternal life.*
[17]*God did not send his Son into the world to condemn it, but to save it.*

Ephesians 2:4-10 (TLB) 4 But God is so rich in mercy; he loved us so much
5 that even though we were spiritually dead and doomed by our

sins, he gave us back our lives again when he raised Christ from the dead – only by his undeserved favor have we ever been saved –

6 and lifted us up from the grave into glory along with Christ, where we sit with him in the heavenly realms – all because of what Christ Jesus did.

7 And now God can always point to us as examples of how very, very rich his kindness is, as shown in all he has done for us through Jesus Christ.

8 Because of his kindness, you have been saved through trusting Christ. And even trusting is not of yourselves; it too is a gift from God.

9 Salvation is not a reward for the good we have done, so none of us can take any credit for it.

10 It is God himself who has made us what we are and given us new lives from Christ Jesus; and long ages ago he planned that we should spend these lives in helping others.

Matthew 13:43 (NLT) Then the righteous will shine like the sun in their Father's Kingdom. Anyone with ears to hear should listen and understand!

Do you need to move from
not knowing to knowing?

Do you need to move from
not doing to doing?

Are you ready for the third move, from this
earth to heaven?

ONE

THE STARTING POINT

John 3:3(TLB): Jesus said, "With all the earnestness I possess I tell you this: Unless you are born again, you can never get into the Kingdom of God."

Some of you may be wondering why you have such a hard time living the Christian life. You know what is right and you agree with it. You go to church, you pray, and you read the Bible. However, you just cannot get it all pulled together. You are a very religious person in many ways, but something seems to be missing.

I want to start with your beginning, your birthday.

I believe there are a great number of persons who believe they are Christians and ready for heaven but live too much of the time in ways that are not righteous or acceptable to God. They try, but they fail. They fail because they are trying to do it on their own.

Here may be the problem. They cannot live a righteous lifestyle because they have never established a relationship with Jesus Christ – been born again.

They **thought** they did when they performed some religious rituals, but they were never really born again. They never became a Christian to start with, they just became religious.

YOU CANNOT BE… UNTIL YOU BECOME!

Think that one over for a while. There has to be a beginning point. I cannot be a student in a specific University until I do what I have to do to become a student. I cannot be a Doctor until I become a Doctor. You cannot be a Christian until you do what you have to do to become a Christian.

You may have gone to church all your life. You may have been born into a Christian home. You may have served or are presently serving in a position in your local church. You try to be an upright and honest citizen. But when you are faced with making right spiritual choices, you often fail because you are still living in the first birth only.

The first birth is of the flesh, born on this earth, born of two human parents. You live a fleshly and material life here on this earth and then you die and your family and friends bury or burn your body. That is not the end! There is more!

In addition to this earthly – fleshly birth, you also have the option of another birth, a second birth. The second birth is also known as being "born again". Some call it being "born from above", "born of the spirit", or "a spiritual birth". This birth from above, this spiritual birth, is something far beyond the fleshly, earthly birth, a birth that cannot be seen, but can be experienced.

It does not change the outside but it does change the inside. You cannot see it but you can see what it does. You can see a difference in the way you live.

The first birth – the fleshly birth

The body

- The body is *amoral*; it is neither evil nor righteous. It is physical – bones, skin, blood, flesh.
- The body is *imperfectible*; it can never be made perfect.
- The body is *mortal*; it has an ending, it will die.

The soul

The soul is tri-functional.
- We have a *mind.* We can *think* about people, ideas, and things.
- We have *emotions.* We can have *feelings* about people, ideas, and things.
- We have a *will*. We can choose, act, and make a decision in relationship to people, ideas, and things, based on our *thinking* and *feeling*.

Examples
- "I *think* that is a good idea and I have decided I *will* do that."
- "I *feel* good about that and I *think* I should *do* it."

It must also be noted that the soul functions are

- *Amoral* – the ability to think, feel, choose, and act is neither good nor evil.
- *Imperfectible* –we will never be perfect in our thinking, feelings or choosing – we are human – only God is perfect.
- *Mortal* – when the body dies, our ability to think, feel and choose, dies also.

Please understand that if you claim to be a Christian, this does not give you license to sin and then excuse it by rambling on about the body, the mind, the will and the emotions not being perfectible. You cannot rationalize that you were operating in the mind, will, and/or emotions and you could not help it, because you were born with these imperfections. It will be best to recognize the sinful behavior as it is and make changes.

When you are still living in the first birth only, you are right; you cannot do anything different – you do not have an option because you are operating under the power, control of the "old man" – the carnal – sinful nature.

There will be times when the body, mind, emotions, and will, fail because you are human. That is a totally different situation than intentionally being disobedient to God's will for you. You may be able to rationalize and lie to yourself and others, but God knows your heart.

The spirit

This is the inner part of us that we cannot see or touch. It is the central part of our being, the control center of our life with God. This is our invisible, untouchable, part that allows us to communicate and connect with God. It is the supernatural part of us. When God made us, he gave us physical bodies, and placed a spirit at the center of our being. This part of us has to do with motive and intent.

We call it our heart, but it is a different heart than the physical heart. Only God can work on this heart. You have heard people say, "In your heart you know..." They are saying at the center of your conscience, your sense of right and wrong, you know..."

The Spirit is _moral_ – that is where you make morally right or wrong decisions.

The Spirit is _perfectible_ – the body, the mind, and emotions will never be perfect, but we can be perfect in spirit. Our intent can be perfect while we fail in our behavior. What I said may have hurt someone, but it was not intentional. The spirit was perfect, the flesh failed. The spirit cannot be made perfect without allowing God to take charge of it. In and of the human, it cannot be made perfect.

We need to be careful at this point and not rationalize or excuse our wrongful behavior and say our intentions were perfect. God knows the truth, and we need to make sure we are telling ourselves and others the truth at this point. There is great danger when we start deceiving ourselves!

It is OK to be wrong, to fail, that is human, a result of our imperfectible soul functions. It is not OK to deny it, lie about it, and refuse to live up to our failure. We need to seek forgiveness, and correct our wrongs.

The Spirit is _immortal_ – it lives on after the body and soul functions die.

> ➤ *Think of situations where the imperfectible soul functions may fail while the perfectible spirit is good.*

The second birth – the spiritual birth

The second birth is of the Spirit and it happens in the spiritual part of our being, the part of man that is not seen but is obviously there. Even people who deny God's existence recognize and talk about the unseen, the mystical, the supernatural part of mankind.

The body and its functions are fascinating. Paul Brand and Phillip Yancey wrote a book about the fleshly body, "Fearfully and Wonderfully Made". It is a good read and I recommend it. The human body is amazing, almost beyond believable.

The soul functions are even more amazing. Just spend a few minutes thinking about thinking. How can we even begin to explain how we can remember what happened to us 40 years ago and instantly smell, feel and experience that event as if it just happened a few moments ago?

Neither the body nor the soul functions can compare to the spiritual life.

Maybe that is why at times we refer to it as the supernatural. It is beyond human understanding. It is a God thing. It blows the human mind. It is beyond comprehension. It cannot be understood by the limited imperfect mind.

The spiritual birth leads to greater living experiences here on earth. It is an inward life that affects our outward living on a daily basis. It eventually leads to endless living (eternal life with God) in a new and perfect spiritual body that we cannot even come close to comprehending in this life.

If you have to understand it to accept it, you will never have it. It is a faith issue.

Ephesians 2:8 (NIV) 8 For it is by grace you have been saved, through faith--and this not from yourselves, it is the gift of God--

Ephesians 2:8 (TLB) 8 Because of his kindness, you have been saved through trusting Christ. And even trusting is not of yourselves; it too is a gift from God.

John 3:3(TLB): Jesus said, "With all the earnestness I possess I tell you this: Unless you are born again, you can never get into the Kingdom of God."

> *Are you born again? Are you sure?*

If you are, you get to go to heaven. It is not a fairy tale story; it is not like Santa Claus, **_HEAVEN IS REAL_**!

In heaven, you will get a new, perfect body that will not have the limitations of this earthly body. It is a second life beyond this life, as we know it here on earth. It is a new, perfect body that will never grow old. It is not like the old, disposable bodies that we have here on this earth.

The fleshly first birth is of this world. The spiritual second birth is from heaven and can only come through Christ and the Spirit of God. **_The born again life,_** the spiritual birth **_can only come through repentance_**.

The new birth, the spiritual birth takes place when you come to Christ and repent. That is, you acknowledge you are a sinner and cannot do anything about it by yourself alone, so you ask Christ to accept you, forgive you, and adopt you – making you a part of God's family.

The born-again life is not deciding to turn over a new leaf and live a better life or join a church. It is not a decision to be a better person. It is not going to church regularly. Nothing we can do will give us this spiritual birth except to repent.

Step one - Realize you are a sinner.

You will feel conviction, condemnation, and/or guilt. In some way, you will sense something is wrong in your life and the way you are living. God is faithful and He will not let you go through life without letting you know that you are not living as He wants you to live. You will realize that you are not righteous; you are not the person God wants you to be. God is making Himself known to you and offering you a gift – the gift of eternal life.

You sense that the way you are living is not pleasing to God. Instead, you are sinful and living in a way that is opposite of God's holiness and righteousness. In short, you are a sinner and need someone to rescue you from your helpless and self-destructive condition.

You are fully aware of the fact that you are a sinner. The Spirit of God has made you aware of your sinful living, via a friend, a preacher, a teacher, or a family member. Maybe it was something you heard or read. Maybe God just made you aware of your condition via His Holy Spirit.

At this point in your life, it becomes your responsibility to do something about it. It doesn't matter how you became aware of your sinful condition. Once you understand that you are a sinner, you have to make a decision. What are you going to do with what you know? Your soul functions – mind, emotions, and will – are called into play. You are thinking about this and you may or you may not have an emotional experience. Some people do and some do not.

You will do something; you will have a positive response or a negative response. Some of you will say you aren't ready to respond or make a decision. By not making a positive response, you have made a decision to remain in your sinful condition, which is a negative response.

At an annual physical checkup, the tests reveal that the patient has cancer but it is in the early stages and with immediate surgery and treatment, the cancer can be stopped. The patient has become aware of his physical condition and has to make a decision about what he is going to do.

The patient will use all three of his soul functions to make a physical decision. He can ignore it and pretend everything is OK. He can deny it and say the doctor is wrong. He can say he will think about it. He can say he does not care and he will just live with it, understanding the final consequences. He can say, "OK, fix me doctor". A doctor cannot force a patient to accept treatment. It is the patient's responsibility to do something.

The same is true when you discover you are a sinner, the moment you are confronted and feel conviction or guilt. You know something is wrong with the way you are living; it becomes your responsibility to do something about it.

You can…

- Deny it – and say it isn't true, you do not believe that stuff.
- Reject it because you do not want to change the way you are living.
- Say you do not understand, and you may not… that is where faith comes in.
- Confess your sinful condition and seek God's forgiveness.

> ➢ *It's your call, what will you do?*

There it is… two choices, you use your mental ability to think and choose.

- You accept God through Jesus Christ and change the way you are living.
- You reject God and suffer the consequences.

Those are the only two choices. You say…

- "Yes, God" or
- "No, God"

If you say, "Yes, God", that is the beginning of repentance. You are now aware that something is not right and you want to fix it. You become aware of a need for a change in your life and your living.

It is like you are coming out of a deep sleep and you are seeing the real you, a person that you have not seen before. It is like going to the doctor and hearing the words, "You have cancer." The way you think and feel about life has suddenly changed; you are beginning to see yourself in the light of God. You are beginning to see the sinful person that you are and you regret the way you have been living and offending God.

Romans 3:23 (TLB) "Yes, all have sinned; all fall short of God's glorious ideal…"

Step two - Confess your belief in Jesus Christ.

You have broken the back of your pride and you can now admit you are a sinner that needs help. You fully understand the only place to get help is Jesus Christ. You confess your belief in Christ as the Son of God and your belief that His death on the cross is payment for your sins.

John 3:16-17 (NIV) "For God so loved the world that he gave his one and only Son, that whoever believes in him shall not perish but have eternal life.
17 For God did not send his Son into the world to condemn the world, but to save the world through him.

Romans 3:24 [TLB] "yet now God declares us "not guilty" of offending him if we trust in Jesus Christ, who in his kindness freely takes away our sins.

Step three – Confess to God your sinful condition and seek His forgiveness.

- Recognize you have a problem you alone cannot fix.
- Admit your need to be fixed.
- Believe you have found the One who can fix your problem.
- Seek forgiveness for your wrongs, your sinful life.

This may be a difficult assignment for some of you because it has always been difficult for you to admit failure – say you were wrong, much less say you are sorry and ask for help. Saying I need someone else's help is admitting I have a problem that is bigger than I am, and I cannot fix it.

➢ *Do you have a problem admitting it when you know you are wrong? Think about it before you move on. This is a big problem for a whole lot of people. Are you one of them?*

To be born again we have to come to the place where we admit we are sinners and we need someone to fix us. That person is Jesus Christ, but He cannot fix us until we admit we need Him to and want Him to fix us.

1 John 1:8-10 (TLB) 8 If we say that we have no sin, we are only fooling ourselves and refusing to accept the truth.
9 But if we confess our sins to him, he can be depended on to forgive us and to cleanse us from every wrong. [And it is perfectly proper for God to do this for us because Christ died to wash away our sins.]

10 If we claim we have not sinned, we are lying and calling God a liar, for he says we have sinned.

Step four – Trust Christ and accept His forgiveness by faith.

Galatians 2:16 (MSG) 16 We know very well that we are not set right with God by rule-keeping but only through personal faith in Jesus Christ. How do we know? We tried it – and we had the best system of rules the world has ever seen! Convinced that no human being can please God by self-improvement, we believed in Jesus as the Messiah so that we might be set right before God by trusting in the Messiah, not by trying to be good.

Galatians 3:24-26 (TLB) 24 Let me put it another way. The Jewish laws were our teacher and guide until Christ came to give us right standing with God through our faith.
25 But now that Christ has come, we do not need those laws any longer to guard us and lead us to him.
26 For now we are all children of God THROUGH FAITH in Jesus Christ,

Ephesians 2:4-10 (NIV) 4 But because of his great love for us, God, who is rich in mercy,
5 made us alive with Christ even when we were dead in transgressions--it is by grace you have been saved.
6 And God raised us up with Christ and seated us with him in the heavenly realms in Christ Jesus,
7 in order that in the coming ages he might show the incomparable riches of his grace, expressed in his kindness to us in Christ Jesus.
8 For it is by grace you have been saved, through faith--and this not from yourselves, it is the gift of God--

9 not by works, so that no one can boast.
10 For we are God's workmanship, created in Christ Jesus to do good works, which God prepared in advance for us to do.

- Believe that He is the Son of God by the way of a miraculous birth.
- Believe He died on the cross.
- Believe He was resurrected from the dead.
- Believe this was payment for our sins if we are willing to accept it.
- Believe in Him enough to trust Him.

Christ was born for the purpose of dying to wash away, forgive, cover our sins. He was miraculously raised from the dead and lives today. This was God's way of rescuing us from our sinful ways.

➢ *Do you believe that?*

To those who can only believe in things that make sense, it is a good story and that is all it is. But if we really believe it, if it is a part of our belief system, we are saved from having to pay for our own sins with our death – not physical death, but spiritual and eternal death.

Because of Christ, we can have eternal life after our earthly death. We were spiritually dead and doomed because of our sins, but because of God's love, mercy, grace, patience, and kindness, He forgave us through Christ's death and resurrection.

Look at Eph. 2:4-10 in The Living Bible.

Ephesians 2:4-10 (TLB)
4 But God is so rich in mercy; he loved us so much
5 that even though we were spiritually dead and doomed by our sins, he gave us back our lives again when he raised Christ from the dead – only by his undeserved favor have we ever been saved –
6 and lifted us up from the grave into glory along with Christ,

where we sit with him in the heavenly realms — all because of what Christ Jesus did.

[7] And now God can always point to us as examples of how very, very rich his kindness is, as shown in all he has done for us through Jesus Christ.

[8] Because of his kindness, you have been saved through trusting Christ. And even trusting is not of yourselves; it too is a gift from God.

[9] Salvation is not a reward for the good we have done, so none of us can take any credit for it.

[10] It is God himself who has made us what we are and given us new lives from Christ Jesus; and long ages ago he planned that we should spend these lives in helping others.

If you have confessed – admitted – acknowledged – that you are a sinner and need forgiveness and you believe Christ is the answer and you make a commitment to follow Him, ***YOU ARE BORN AGAIN***.

You will still face a physical death because you were born physically, but you will live on forever with God in your new body that your spirit will occupy in heaven.

Accept the forgiveness by faith. Then prove you are born again – a new person in Christ by intentionally, purposefully changing the way you live. Christ is in you and you are in Him. Show that by your actions. Be faithful to the end and you will receive the big prize – eternal life with Christ.

Step five – Commit to thinking and living differently.

➤ *Do you want to think and live differently? Do you really want to be a different person than what you are now?*

You must commit to be obedient to all of Christ's teachings. You are saying yes to God. This is the final step in repentance. If you do not agree to follow the teachings of Christ, your repentance is not complete. You must follow the teachings of the Bible. In my opinion, Romans 12 may be the single most important chapter in the whole Bible for new Christians. It clearly tells us how we are to live after we are born again. It starts out by requiring a complete and full commitment to be all and do all you will ever know God wants you to be and do.

When you become a follower of Christ, you will most likely need to make some serious changes in the way you live. Follow all the instructions available to you in this chapter for righteous living and you will become a brand new person.

The change will start on the inside – agreeing with God – in the spiritual part of your life, the part that cannot be seen. This change will affect the way you approach everything in life. You will have new Priorities, which will change your Attitude. New Priorities and new Attitude will help create greater Discipline and Determination to do what is right – to follow God's instructions for living.

When this dynamic all comes together,

- You will experience for yourself what real living is all about.
- You will discover true happiness and satisfaction in life.
- You will have a new passion.
- Your new passion will drive your imperfect mind, emotions, and will, in a new direction.
- You will have a desire to learn more about God.
- You will experience new emotions that you have never had.
- You will make better choices than you have ever made.

This is what you are to do!

*Romans 12:1-2 (MSG) 1 So here's what I want you to do, God helping you: Take your everyday, ordinary life – your sleeping, eating, going-to-work, and walking-around life – and place it before God as an offering. Embracing what God does for you is the best thing you can do for him. (**That is a big commitment on your part.**)*

2 Do not become so well-adjusted to your culture that you fit into it without even thinking. Instead, fix your attention on God. You'll be changed from the inside out. Readily recognize what he wants from you, and quickly respond to it. Unlike the culture around you, always dragging you down to its level of immaturity, God brings the best out of you, develops well-formed maturity in you.

Look at the entire chapter from The Living Bible below. Do not just read this; study it, and ask yourself how it applies to you. Ask God to help you see where this identifies your gifts, talents, abilities. Get these thoughts planted in your mind.

➤ *At this point, what do you think your gifts, talents, abilities may be when it comes to serving God? Just do your best; list them. This is not your final list. It is a starting point in determining how you are going to serve God.*

If you are going to live the Christian life, these ways will become your ways. This is where the renewing of the mind begins. You will begin to develop your _Priority_ list in a way that will be pleasing to God. This is a vital point in your becoming a new wonderful person. You have to want your priorities to be the same as God's priorities.

➤ *Later in this book, I will ask you to review your list of gifts, talents, abilities that best fit you. You may make some changes from the list you just made. I will ask you to make a mental and physical commitment to start doing the things that you have the ability to do. That will help you develop an _Attitude_ like that of Christ.*

Romans 12:1-21 (TLB) 1 And so, dear brothers, I plead with you to give your bodies to God. Let them be a living sacrifice, holy – the kind he can accept. When you think of what he has done for you, is this too much to ask?

2 Do not copy the behavior and customs of this world, but be a new and different person with a fresh newness in all you do and think. Then you will learn from your own experience how his ways will really satisfy you.

3 As God's messenger I give each of you God's warning: Be honest in your estimate of yourselves, measuring your value by how much faith God has given you.

4 Just as there are many parts to our bodies, so it is with Christ's body.

5 We are all parts of it, and it takes every one of us to make it complete, for we each have different work to do. So we belong to each other, and each needs all the others.

6 God has given each of us the ability to do certain things well. So if God has given you the ability to prophesy, then prophesy whenever you can – as often as your faith is strong enough to receive a message from God.

7 If your gift is that of serving others, serve them well. If you are a teacher, do a good job of teaching.

8 If you are a preacher, see to it that your sermons are strong and helpful. If God has given you money, be generous in helping others with it. If God has given you administrative ability and put you in charge of the work of others, take the responsibility seriously. Those who offer comfort to the sorrowing should do so with Christian cheer.

9 Do not just pretend that you love others: really love them. Hate what is wrong. Stand on the side of the good.

10 Love each other with brotherly affection and take delight in honoring each other.

11 Never be lazy in your work, but serve the Lord enthusiastically.

12 Be glad for all God is planning for you. Be patient in trouble, and prayerful always.

13 When God's children are in need, you be the one to help them out. And get into the habit of inviting guests home for dinner or, if they need lodging, for the night.

14 If someone mistreats you because you are a Christian, do not curse him; pray that God will bless him.

15 When others are happy, be happy with them. If they are sad, share their sorrow.

16 Work happily together. Do not try to act big. Do not try to get into the good graces of important people, but enjoy the company of ordinary folks. And do not think you know it all!

17 Never pay back evil for evil. Do things in such a way that everyone can see you are honest clear through.

18 Do not quarrel with anyone. Be at peace with everyone, just as much as possible.

19 Dear friends, never avenge yourselves. Leave that to God, for he has said that he will repay those who deserve it. [Do not take the law into your own hands.]

20 Instead, feed your enemy if he is hungry. If he is thirsty give him something to drink and you will be "heaping coals of fire on his head." In other words, he will feel ashamed of himself for what he has done to you.

21 Do not let evil get the upper hand, but conquer evil by doing good.

Before you have finished this book, you will have encountered parts of this chapter several times. That is intentional. The more times these thoughts pass through your mind, the more likely they will replay in your mind when they can be helpful. The Bible says that we are to saturate our minds with the word of God.

2 Timothy 2:19 (TLB) 19 But God's truth stands firm like a great rock, and nothing can shake it. It is a foundation stone with these words written on it: "The Lord knows those who are really his," and "A person who calls himself a Christian should not be doing things that are wrong".

II Timothy 3:16-17 (TLB) 16 The whole Bible was given to us by inspiration from God and is useful to teach us what is true and to make us realize what is wrong in our lives; it straightens us out and helps us do what is right.

17 It is God's way of making us well prepared at every point, fully equipped to do good to everyone.

If you are born again, you are becoming a changed person, a new person, because you are converted – you will no longer want to live the way you used to live.

If there is no change in your living, there is no new birth. If you haven't changed, you are the same person you were before you went through those religious rituals – that is all they were to you. There was no genuine experience with Christ.

I am spending extra time here because it seems so many who say they are born again – say they are Christians, do not understand that they will not continue to sin if they are truly born again. They cannot just say, "I believe in Jesus" and continue living in sin.

1 John 3:4-10 (NIV) 4 Everyone who sins breaks the law; in fact, sin is lawlessness. 5 But you know that he appeared so that he might take away our sins. And in him is no sin.
6 No one who lives in him keeps on sinning. No one who continues to sin has either seen him or known him.
7 Dear children, do not let anyone lead you astray. He who does what is right is righteous, just as he is righteous.
8 He who does what is sinful is of the devil, because the devil has been sinning from the beginning. The reason the Son of God appeared was to destroy the devil's work.
9 No one who is born of God will continue to sin, because God's seed remains in him; he cannot go on sinning, because he has been born of God.
10 This is how we know who the children of God are and who the children of the devil are: Anyone who does not do what is right is not a child of God; nor is anyone who does not love his brother.

1 John 5:18 (NIV) "We know that anyone born of God does not continue to sin; the one who was born of God keeps him safe, and the evil one cannot harm him."

Recently someone sent me an e-mail telling about a man that claimed to have accepted Christ because he wanted to go to heaven. When confronted with his obvious continual sinful behavior, his response was that he did not know he had to quit sinning after he accepted Christ.

Because you are a new and different person, you will start thinking differently. If you have had a true conversion, you will still be tempted to do wrong, but the spirit of God that now lives in you will remind you of how you are supposed to live. The perfectible spirit sends a message to the imperfectible mind.

John 14:26 (TLB) But when the Father sends the Comforter instead of me – and by the Comforter I mean the Holy Spirit – he will teach you much, as well as remind you of everything I myself have told you.

When you are born again, you will have a desire to live like God wants you to live, not like you were living before you came to God. You consciously, purposefully, intentionally choose to live differently than you had been living. You change directions in attitude and living styles. You choose to stop sinning. You make a conscious choice not to participate in the things of the world that are unrighteous and displeasing to God.

WHEN YOU ARE BORN AGAIN YOU FEEL COMPELLED TO LIVE A DIFFERENT LIFESTYLE.

If you do not have a desire to do what Jesus teaches, you have not been born again. Christ is not in you! When Christ comes into your life, it changes the way you think.

Do not be fooled. Satan will not stand aside and let you go without a fight. You will most likely have times when your spirit is strong – your desire to do right is strong, but in the human, you fail. Do not let Satan defeat you at this point and tell you that all this is just stuff and means nothing. You are still human and subject to temptation and failure.

When you do fail, do not just brush that failure aside and make some excuse. Immediately turn to God and tell him that you are aware that you just failed, seek His forgiveness, ask for added strength and faith to continue in your walk, in your new life with Christ.

Step six – Finalize the deal.

It is important that you follow through by telling others that you have accepted Christ as your Savior, have received forgiveness of your sins, and have made a decision to follow Him.

> *Romans 10:9-10 (TLB) "For if you tell others with your own mouth that Jesus Christ is your Lord and believe in your own heart that God has raised him from the dead, you will be saved. 10 For it is by believing in his heart that a man becomes right with God; and with his mouth he tells others of his faith, confirming his salvation.*

> *Matthew 10:32-33 (TLB) 32 "If anyone publicly acknowledges me as his friend, I will openly acknowledge him as my friend before my Father in heaven.*
> *33 But if anyone publicly denies me, I will openly deny him before my Father in heaven.*

Christ told his followers to share their new relationship with others. What would make us think that we are to do less? We become one of His disciples when we repent and turn from our sins. God wants to use us to bring others to Him.

Mark 16:15-16 (MSG) 15 Then he said, "Go into the world. Go everywhere and announce the Message of God's good news to one and all.
16 Whoever believes and is baptized is saved; whoever refuses to believe is damned.

Step seven – Be blessed – refreshed.

The refreshing will be a better life, a cleaner life, a fresh life, a blessed life, a free life.

When I was a youth pastor, I tried to make it a pattern to pick up two or three kids after school and go for a Coke and visit, or just ride around.

One particular time I had picked up a high school football star. The guys loved my Ford pickup and I would let them drive occasionally, which made their day and sometimes wrecked my nerves.

I remember it as if it were last week every time I drive down Tuxedo Blvd in Bartlesville, Oklahoma, and pass a certain spot. After riding around for a while, I talked to him about his relationship with Christ. He prayed to accept Christ while we were driving around. Afterwards he looked at me and said something like this, "I feel so clean on the inside!" He was feeling refreshed and blessed. He was feeling like a new person.

➢ *Would you like to feel refreshed and blessed?*

Acts 3:19[NIV] "Repent then and turn to God so that your sins may be wiped out, that times of refreshing may come from the Lord."

Acts 3:19 [TLB] Now change your mind and attitude to God and turn to him so he can cleanse away your sins and send you wonderful times of refreshment from the presence of the Lord.

Notice the **"SO HE CAN"**. What does that mean? It means we must do something before GOD can do what He wants to do. We have to change before God can pour out His blessings on us. We have to have a connection with Him. We cannot just have a mental knowledge of Him. There has to be a spiritual connection.

Life Application Study Bible

Acts 3:19, 20 "When we repent, God promises not only to wipe out our sins, but to bring spiritual refreshment. Repentance may at first seem painful because it is hard to give up certain sins."

The Amplified Bible for the same verses says,

"So repent - change your mind and purpose; turn around and return [to God], that your sins may be erased (blotted out, wiped clean), that times of refreshing - of recovering from the effects of heat, of reviving with fresh air - may come from the presence of the Lord."

Romans 5:1 (NIV) [1] Therefore, since we have been justified through faith, we have peace with God through our Lord Jesus Christ,

I am confident that every living person at some point in their life has a desire for a time of refreshing, a fresh starting over that brings on the good feelings, the contentment, the true and full satisfaction in life.

2 Chronicles 7:14 (NIV) [14] *if my people, who are called by my name, will humble themselves and pray and seek my face and turn from their wicked ways, then will I hear from heaven and will forgive their sin and will heal their land.*

Could it be, if professing Christians would humble themselves and repent, and seek God and turn from their wicked ways as God has told them to do, we would discover the answer to our nation's problems as well?

Some people want to do things their way and expect God to bless, revive, and refresh them, in spite of their rejection of God's ways for their lives.

It would be as logical for us to expect our employers to give us time off, give us a promotion, give us a raise, and make everything good for us in spite of the fact that we disregard their instructions and do what we want, when we want.

The *Life Application Study Bible* says about II Chronicles 7:14.

"In chapter 6, Solomon asked God to make provisions for the people when they sinned. God answered with four conditions for forgiveness:

(1) Humble yourself by admitting your sins,

(2) Pray to God, asking for forgiveness,

(3) Seek God continually, and

(4) Turn from sinful behavior.

True repentance is more than talk — it is changed behavior. Whether we sin individually, as a group, or as a nation, following these steps will lead to forgiveness. God will answer our earnest prayers."

The blessings from the Lord will follow repentance.

Deuteronomy 28:1-6 (TLB) [1] *"If you fully obey all of these commandments of the Lord your God, the laws I am declaring to you today, God will transform you into the greatest nation in the world.*

[2] *These are the blessings that will come upon you:*

[3] *Blessings in the city, Blessings in the field;*

[4] *Many children, Ample crops, Large flocks and herds;*

[5] *Blessings of fruit and bread;*

[6] *Blessings when you come in, Blessings when you go out.*

TWO

THE TRANSFORMATION

The old you

Before you become a Christian, you do not have a choice of how you will live because you are a sinner from birth, and you are born with a carnal – anti-God – nature. When Satan sets a trap, you take it, usually without even thinking anything of it because it is your nature to do evil. It is a way of life for you, a way God does not want you to live.

In the following scripture - (Gal 5:19), you read, **_"But when you follow your own wrong inclinations_"**. That means you are inclined, motivated, liable to do a certain thing a certain way because that is the natural, normal, acceptable way for you to do that particular thing. When you are tempted to sin, you sin because that is what your nature says you should do. The sad thing is you have no choice – you are under the control of your sinful nature.

> Galatians 5:19-21 (TLB) 19 But when you follow your own
> wrong inclinations, your lives will produce these evil results:
> Impure thoughts, eagerness for lustful pleasure,
> 20 idolatry, spiritism (that is, encouraging the activity of
> demons), hatred and fighting, jealousy and anger, constant effort
> to get the best for yourself, complaints and criticisms, the feeling
> that everyone else is wrong except those in your own little
> group – and there will be wrong doctrine,
> 21 envy, murder, drunkenness, wild parties, and all that sort of

thing. Let me tell you again, as I have before, that anyone living that sort of life will not inherit the Kingdom of God.

I have great concern about the number of individuals who say they are followers of Christ that are involved in "lustful pleasure" – "sexual immorality" – pornography, and do not seem to think it is wrong and unacceptable to God. Pornography definitely is "lustful pleasure." Pornography is one of the most damaging habits one can have. It can set you up for activities that you will later regret. It can cost you your marriage.

➢ *If this applies to you, I would encourage you, for your own good, to check it out. Do some Biblical research and see if you can find anything that even indicates "lustful pleasure" – "sexual immorality" is acceptable behavior for one that is a follower of Christ.*

Following are some scriptures that boldly speak against it.

Mark 7:20-21 (NIV) [20] *He (Jesus) went on: "What comes out of a man is what makes him 'unclean.'*
[21]*For from within, out of men's hearts, come evil thoughts, sexual immorality, theft, murder, adultery,..."*

Romans 1:28-29 (NKJV) [28] *And even as they did not like to retain God in their knowledge, God gave them over to a debased mind, to do those things which are not fitting;*
[29] *being filled with all unrighteousness, sexual immorality, wickedness, covetousness, maliciousness; full of envy, murder, strife, deceit, evil-mindedness; they are whisperers,...*

Galatians 5:19 (NLT) [19]*When you follow the desires of your sinful nature, the results are very clear: sexual immorality, impurity, lustful pleasures,...*

1 Thessalonians 4:3 (NIV) [3] *It is God's will that you should be sanctified: that you should avoid sexual immorality;*

Lying is another behavior that seems to have become acceptable behavior to professing followers of Christ.

Revelation 21:8 (NIV) *⁸ But the cowardly, the unbelieving, the vile, the murderers, the sexually immoral, those who practice magic arts, the idolaters and all liars--their place will be in the fiery lake of burning sulfur. This is the second death."*

Please notice *"sexual immorality"* and *"lustful pleasures"* and *"liars"* are in the same list as theft, murder, and adultery." These things are not acceptable to God.

Notice what it says about your future in following your wrong inclinations, (Galatians 5:21) "***anyone living that sort of life will not inherit the Kingdom of God***." That means you do not go to heaven. Before you repent and turn to Christ you cannot avoid the traps – sin, it is your way of life. After you repent, you become a new person with new options.

The new you

Ephesians 4:22-24 (TLB) *²² then throw off your old evil nature – the old you that was a partner in your evil ways – rotten through and through, full of lust and sham.*
²³ Now your attitudes and thoughts must all be constantly changing for the better.
²⁴ Yes, you must be a new and different person, holy and good. Clothe yourself with this new nature.

When we repent, we become a new person in Christ. That means; if we choose to, we can follow the ways of Christ instead of the ways of Satan. We can avoid the traps. We now have an option. This is not an automatic change, where we do not have to do anything. It does not just happen. We do not become dummies controlled by a stick and string. We are involved mentally and emotionally. Our soul functions become active. We think, we feel, and we choose.

As followers of Christ, we have the ability to be different and avoid the traps. We can change directions in the way we are going. We have a choice – we have to choose to be different. As we discipline ourselves, we receive assistance from the Holy Spirit.

If you are already serving Satan, he doesn't need to set a camouflaged trap for you, he just needs to keep feeding you, making available to you the things he knows you like, the things that give you temporary gratification, that makes you feel good for the moment." This is just a way of life for the "old man" – the sinner.

After you repent and become a Christ follower, you become a new person and God sends His Holy Spirit to assist you in living the new life, which means you can now avoid the traps.

> Galatians 5:22-26 (TLB) 22 But when the holy spirit controls our lives he will produce this kind of fruit in us: love, joy, peace, patience, kindness, goodness, faithfulness,
> 23 gentleness and self-control; and here there is no conflict with Jewish laws.
> 24 Those who belong to Christ have nailed their natural evil desires to his cross and crucified them there.
> 25 If we are living now by the Holy Spirit's power, let us follow the Holy Spirit's leading in every part of our lives.
> 26 Then we will not need to look for honors and popularity, which lead to jealousy and hard feelings.

Wow, that is quite different from the way we lived as a follower of Satan (the "old Man") caught up in every trap he sets. We do not have to be under the control of the old person. We can be free from that if we want to be free from it. We will still be tempted. Satan will still set the traps, but we can choose to avoid them. We see a better way, and we choose to take the better way. We have the ability to say "no" to the traps.

To learn the ways of the new person, we have to read and study the Bible. Become involved in Bible studies. Hang out with people who will help you learn the ways of Christ and assist you along the way.

I cannot just decide I want to be a medical doctor and open up shop. I have to go to school, read the books, hang out with others that are on the same path and learn from them. It is a determined way of life. You have to develop an attitude that says, "I am going to do this".

Being a Christian, following Christ and making sure you are ready to go to heaven at any given time in your life is an intentional, on purpose, determined way of life. You keep learning and growing every day. You have to fill your mind constantly with the teachings and the ways of Christ so you can quickly recognize the traps and avoid them. As you spend time reading and learning about the ways of Christ, you become strong in the Lord, making it easier to avoid the traps.

Learn to use the **"PADD"**

You get your **Priorities** straight. Find out what God thinks and feels about things. Find out what God says is important and make that important to you. Make obeying and pleasing God your most important priority. Make it your ultimate priority. Follow His lead in placing values on things, people, and actions.

You develop a new and better **Attitude.** You start thinking and feeling like God thinks and feels about things. This transformed mind redirects the way you think and feel about everything, which will change what you do and do not do.

> *Read and study the Proverbs to help you with setting your priorities and developing a right attitude.*

You begin to **Discipline** yourself. You make yourself do what you know is right just because it is right. Do what you know and know what you do… IS RIGHT!

You become very **Determined**, strong-minded, single-minded, unwavering in your drive to live the way God wants you to live. Nothing is going to get in the way of your loving and serving God.

> *Romans 12:1(TLB) "And so, dear brothers, I plead with you to give your bodies to God. Let them be a living sacrifice, holy – the kind he can accept. When you think of what he has done for you, is this too much to ask?"*

That does not sound like it is done for you, it sounds like you have to make some choices and discipline yourself – make yourself do it.

> *You can learn more about this analogy of the old person and the new person by reading the entire books of Galatians and Ephesians found in the New Testament. They are short books. Take time to read them now.*

The natural carnal traits that create our physical, mental, and emotional appetites do not just disappear. They do not just go away when we become Christians as some people mistakenly believe.

We have to replace them with Christ-like traits. We get a mental makeover – our minds are transformed – renewed.

We get a new chance at living right. We may fall like a baby just learning to walk, but we immediately admit we have fallen. We confess our sin to God, seek God's forgiveness, get up and move on.

You plant a garden and then it grows. If you do not plant it, nothing is going to grow. Repentance is planting the garden. The growth, renewal, transforming of the mind, changing the way we think, comes through a learning process known as spiritual growth. Until this happens, you are going to keep getting caught in the traps.

Romans 12, tells us how it happens. It is a gradual process. The initial start is repentance. Then we start the process of transforming the way we think. The more we change the way we think, the more we change the way we live.

> *Romans 12:2 (NIV) "Do not conform any longer to the pattern of this world, but be transformed by the renewing of your mind. Then you will be able to test and approve what God's will is--his good, pleasing and perfect will".*

> *Romans 12:2 (TLB) "Do not copy the behavior and customs of this world, but be a new and different person with a fresh newness in all you do and think. Then you will learn from your own experience how his ways will really satisfy you."*

Look at this carefully, this does not say you cannot act like you used to. It does not say you do not have the ability to live the way you used to live. It does not say the temptation to live like you used to live has been taken away from you.

It gives you a command. YOU – yes, you – **DO NOT** live that way any longer. Quit doing those things you used to do. They are not what God wants in you. Do you not get it? Do you not understand? This is your responsibility – this is your part! You have to learn this new way and then **Discipline** yourself to do what you have learned.

YOU ARE GOING TO CHANGE THE WAY YOU LIVE BY CHANGING THE WAY YOU THINK.

THIS HAPPENS WHEN YOUR PRIORITIES AND YOUR ATTITUDE ARE IN SYNC WITH GOD.

Every time you read the Bible, pray, and search your heart (get close to God), you are re-syncing.

As long as you are looking for satisfaction in the traps, the sinful way you have been living, you are going to go on being unsatisfied. You are never going to get what you are seeking in the traps of Satan. You will never be able to get enough. You are made in God's image and you will never find satisfaction in this life until you start living in His image. You will have temporary gratification and that is all.

You cannot undermine, criticize, slander, lie about someone or something, gossip, find pleasure in sensual things, be angry and fight, steal, etc. enough to be satisfied. You will keep going back for more. That is the genius of Satan's traps. They look good but are never fulfilling.

When your thinking is like God's thinking and your living is the way He wants you to live, you will find life to be:

- Better
- More rewarding
- More pleasant
- More exciting
- More comforting
- More encouraging than anything you find in the traps.

That is the way of the "new man".

LIVING AS GOD WANTS YOU TO LIVE IS JUST A BETTER WAY OF LIFE - GUARANTEED!

When we become this new person, we begin to live Christ-like lives.

Ephesians 4:22-24 (NIV) [22] *You were taught, with regard to your former way of life, to put off your old self, which is being corrupted by its deceitful desires;*

The "*deceitful desires*" that you are "**corrupted by**" are the deceptive traps that look good, sound good, and feel good, but they are killers. They corrupt you; they make you dishonest, crooked, unethical, immoral, shady people. When you get caught in these traps, it changes who you are and starts you out on a trip that looks and sounds good, but you will not like the final destination.

Let me start over.

[22] *You were taught, with regard to your former way of life, to put off your old self, which is being corrupted by its deceitful desires;*
[23] *to be made new in the attitude of your minds;*
[24] *and to put on the new self, created to be like God in true righteousness and holiness.*

Notice the first word in verse 22 "YOU". This is something YOU do. YOU… "put off your old self".

Notice verse 24. YOU… "put on the new self."

This does not say somebody else is going to dress you – do it for you. You have been made a new person and *you are capable of doing this*. God is not going to tell you to do something then make it so hard it is impossible for you to do it. With God's help, you can become a new and different person and avoid the traps of Satan.

This is where the first **D** from the **PADD** comes into play – *Discipline.* The Christian life is not a life for wimps. You have to give it your best and God will help you. If you are playing games and pretending you are giving it your best, that is all you are going to get. God always knows the truth.

> *Philippians 4:13 (TLB) for I can do everything God asks me to with the help of Christ who gives me the strength and power.*

> *Psalm 32:8 (TLB) I will instruct you (says the Lord) and guide you along the best pathway for your life; I will advise you and watch your progress.*

➢ *Who owns you? To whom do you belong? Who do you follow the most – God or Satan?*

➢ *Do you pretend to be a Christian and go to church and pray and sing in the choir and serve on the church board then turn around and slander someone?*

➢ *Do you say you are a Christian, and then lie?*

➢ *Do you go to your small group Bible study, then go home and look at sexual material in an attempt to find sensual gratification?*

➢ *Do you tell your boss you are a Christian then steal eight hours of pay by saying you are sick and then go fishing? Oh, yes, I guess that would be lying to him also, wouldn't it?*

It is a decision you make. This is your responsibility. You can be free from the traps because you have Christ living in you. You can do this by following the ways and teachings of Christ.

➢ *Are you the "old man", making bad decisions, getting caught in one trap after another or are you the "new man", living free from the traps and living for God in everything you do?*

Where you are weak, if you are committed and determined, Christ will give you the extra strength you need to do what you are supposed to do.

Philippians 4:13 (TLB) for I can do everything God asks me to with the help of Christ who gives me the strength and power.

The key is giving ourselves completely, totally to God to use as He wants.

There is a song written by Francis Havergal in 1874. Listen to the words. This is quite opposite of the "old man" who does everything thinking of himself first and foremost – all self-centered acts.

Take my life and let it be
Consecrated, Lord, to Thee.
Take my moments and my days;
Let them flow in endless praise.

Take my hands and let them move
at the impulse of Thy love.
Take my feet and let them be
Swift and beautiful for Thee.

Take my voice and let me sing,
Always, only for my King.
Take my lips and let them be
filled with messages from Thee.

Take my silver and my gold,
not a mite would I withhold.
Take my intellect and use
every pow 'r as Thou shalt choose.

Take my will and make it Thine,
It shall be no longer mine.

Take my heart, it is Thine own,
it shall be Thy royal throne.

Take my love, my God; I pour
At Thy feet its treasure store.
Take myself and I will be
Ever, only, all for Thee.

Live on the "**PADD**"

- Get your ***Priorities*** right – set them by God's standards. Make what God says is the most important, the most important thing to you.
- Take on the ***Attitude*** of Christ – pattern your thinking and feeling after the way He thinks and feels about things. Take on the mind of Christ.
- ***Discipline*** yourself harder than you ever have.
- Be ***Determined,*** single-minded, bull-headed, strong in your drive to do everything you do, God's way.

You can become a new fulfilled – satisfied person.

Romans 12:2 (NIV) "…Then you will be able to test and approve what God's will is--his good, pleasing and perfect will."

Romans 12:2 (TLB)"…Then you will learn from your own experience how his ways will really satisfy you."

Romans 12:2 (MSG) "… God brings the best out of you, develops well-formed maturity in you."

Otherwise, you are on your own. You will be doing what you want to do and you will be limited to what you can gain in the human alone. I guarantee you that will never be enough. You will go on day after day, night after night seeking and seeking and seeking something to satisfy you. Without Christ, you will never find it.

The new you will seek forgiveness in an attempt to right your wrongs.

We are talking about asking someone to forgive you for your wrongful behavior. If you took something from them wrongfully, you need to make restitution.

I am going to spend some extra time with this point because I believe it is a very important part of repentance, and too often overlooked. Maybe avoided would be a better word. Because it is a very hard thing to do, I think people rationalize that they do not really need to do it.

The original word for restitution means:

- To restore
- To compensate
- To set in order again
- To bring back to a former condition or state of being.

Here is what the *Holman Bible Dictionary* says about restitution.

"RESTITUTION: The act of returning what has wrongfully been taken or replacing what has been lost or damaged and the Divine restoration of all things to their original order."

"Human Restitution: "…sins against a neighbor (theft, deception, dishonesty, extortion, keeping lost property, or damaging property). Such crimes involved "unfaithfulness" towards God and disrupted fellowship and peace among the people."

Jesus implicitly validated the practice when he admonished followers to "be reconciled" to a brother before offering a gift to God."

Matthew 5:23-24 (Living): "So if you are standing before the altar in the Temple, offering a sacrifice to God, and suddenly remember that a friend has something against you,
24 leave your sacrifice there beside the altar and go and apologize and be reconciled to him, and then come and offer your sacrifice to God."

Some have said they do not believe it is necessary to make restitution for things like lying to or about someone, slandering, and gossiping, getting angry and raging, or creating division in the church because, *"That is between God and me"*. I think this attitude is too common among professing Christians. Maybe these kinds of behavior have become acceptable because they are the so-called, "little sins."

Bad behavior on your part with the purpose of hurting others, mentally, emotionally, or physically is wrong. It is also being unfaithful to God because He has commanded us not to do those things and to be kind instead. It is my opinion that if we have not followed the commands of God in our relationship with others, we need to make it right with God and others.

Can I find a scripture that says, "If you lied to someone or hurt someone by intentionally saying unkind things to him or about him, you must go seek his forgiveness?" No, I cannot. However, I think it is implied. If God says, it is wrong to do something to hurt people, I think we need to apologize to the one we offended and seek his forgiveness in an attempt to restore the relationship, if we are going to be pleasing to God.

It may be the person you said something to that you need to go to and seek forgiveness. Going to the person you said it about, may create additional problems. They may not even know you have been saying bad things about them. Straighten it up with the person you said it to.

Just recently, I caught myself saying some unkind things to someone about another person. During the night, I believe the Holy Spirit of God connected with my spirit and showed me how wrong I was. I was wrong saying anything that would damage another person's character. The next day I went to my friend and apologized, and sought forgiveness. Doing this is a humbling experience and I think it helps you be more careful in the future.

An additional problem may be that we have now planted thoughts in the mind of another that we cannot erase. We can only pray that God will erase from their mind the thoughts we planted there.

> Proverbs 6:16 (TLB) [16] For there are six things the Lord hates – no, seven: Haughtiness, Lying, Murdering, Plotting evil, Eagerness to do wrong, A false witness, Sowing discord among brothers.

> Ephesians 4:31-32 (TLB) [31] Stop being mean, bad-tempered, and angry. Quarreling, harsh words, and dislike of others should have no place in your lives.
> [32] Instead, be kind to each other, tenderhearted, forgiving one another, just as God has forgiven you because you belong to Christ.

➤ *Who is it you need to ask to forgive you for the wrong you did to them?*

➤ *To whom do you need to make restitution?*

➤ *What are you going to do about these two issues?*

I know there may be situations where it is impossible to make restitution, but we are to do the best we can.

The Holman Bible Dictionary says

> Human Restitution: The Law required "trespass offerings" to be made for sins against a neighbor (theft, deception, dishonesty,

extortion, keeping lost property, or damaging property). Such crimes involved "unfaithfulness" towards God and disrupted fellowship and peace among the people. They were to be atoned for by a guilt offering to God, and "restitution" to the wronged neighbor. Atonement and forgiveness of the sin were received after restitution had been made to the victim. The sin offering to God always followed the act of restitution. Old Testament law established a principle of "punishment to fit the crime" (life for life, eye for eye, tooth for tooth, wound for wound). Restitution was consistent with this concept of equity. The stolen property was to be returned, or "full" compensation was to be made. The guidelines for making complete restitution also included a provision for punitive damages (up to five times what had been lost), justice that moved beyond "an eye for an eye." Provisions were made for complications in this process (Ex. 22:3). The act of making restitution to a victim was so closely identified with the atoning sacrifice made to God, that the two expressions could be seen as elements of the same command. Neither could stand alone. Specific examples of this law in operation are not found, but the principle in action is found (1 Kings 20:34; 2 Kings 8:6; Neh. 5:10-12). There is no legal or ritual application of this command in the New Testament; however, the principle of restitution is clearly pictured in the story of Zacchaeus (Luke 19:1-10). Jesus implicitly validated the practice when he admonished followers to "be reconciled" to a brother before offering a gift to God (Matt. 5:23-24).

The Holy Spirit of God will begin to work in your mind and show where you need to make things right with others. I have a great concern, that we have pushed into the background, shelved, the need to make things right with those we have wronged.

Galatians 5: 25 (TLB):"If we are living now by the Holy Spirit's power, let us follow the Holy Spirit's leading in every part of our lives.

Someone asked, "What if the person you need to reconcile with is dead or you cannot locate them?" We can only do what we can do. When we can do something, I think it is required of us to do it. God's grace takes care of the rest.

This all flashed before me a few years ago, before I felt I should write this book. I felt the need to be reconciled to a particular man. How could I do it? He was dead. I thought I was off the hook. When I was about 21-22 years old, I painted a house for a man. When I finished, I loaded my equipment in my old Ford station wagon, properly named, "The Paint Wagon". I also loaded the leftover paint – less than a gallon. The problem was I did not buy the paint, he did. I took the paint he had bought. It was a very small issue. He probably did not even know I had taken it, probably did not know there was any paint left, and probably did not care.

So why am I being bothered about this 50+ years later? I do not know. I thought about it and decided I could do nothing since he had died many years ago. It kept bothering me. Then I met his grandson – what a coincidence. Now I am facing this half gallon of paint issue again. I finally went to the grandson, told him the story, and handed him what I thought it would cost today to replace the paint. He rejected it and told me to take it to the Salvation Army, and I did. After that, I felt as free as an eagle flying through the sky.

I think people may neglect making restitutions because it is difficult to face someone we know that we have wronged. Is this a pride issue? Does the Bible say pride can be a sin issue? The answer to both questions is "yes".

If there is something that we should make right with someone we have wronged and we are seriously trying to be obedient to God, the Holy Spirit of God will remind us of it.

Ephesians 4:23-24 (TLB) "Now your attitudes and thoughts must all be constantly changing for the better. 24 Yes, you must be a new and different person, holy and good. Clothe yourself with this new nature."

- "Your attitudes and thoughts must all be constantly changing for the better..."
- "You must be a new and different person..."
- That new and different person must be "...holy and good"
- "Clothe yourself with this new nature"

➢ *Would you like to be a new and different person?*

➢ *Can you think of any attitudes and thoughts that you need to change? What are they?*

➢ *Do you know what you need to do to become a new and different person?*

➢ *What will you do to accomplish those things?*

The new birth means you are a new person in Christ, and that means you will be feeling a need not only to do things differently from this point on but also to make things right in areas where you did wrong in the past. You will be thinking and/or feeling, "I do not feel right about what I did or said and I need to go back and fix that".

It just seems natural to me that if I am a new and different person, perfect in spirit – Christ is in me and I am in Him – there would be something in me that makes me want to amend, restore, fix, patch-up, etc. the wrongs of the past. That would include damaging someone's character, and/or causing mental and/or emotional suffering by what I may have said or done. I think I would not want anything in the past, present, or future to be "out of sync" with what God wants me to be. You may suddenly think, "I was wrong when I _____ and I need to go back and make it right."

➢ *What are you thinking about right now that you need to go make right? Are you going to do it or just think about it?*

Galatians 5: 25(TLB): If we are living now by the Holy Spirit's power, let us follow the Holy Spirit's leading in every part of our lives.

The old you was comfortable with wronging others, but the new you cannot be comfortable with wronging others. Neither should you be comfortable with the wrongs of the past. You may suddenly have flashbacks where your heart begins to race, and you begin to have panic attacks and sweaty hands thinking I did or said _____. I need to go make that right.

You are a new person. Christ is in you and you are in Christ. You have something inside you that makes you want to mend fences. It is a new and maybe scary feeling because all of a sudden you do not want to have conflict; you do not want to wrong and hurt others; you do not want to be a problem; you no longer have a desire to create dissension and division in the church, at work, at home or in your neighborhood. You want to make peace, you want to be kind, you want to love and help others. In short, you want to make life better for others and yourself.

I am troubled at the number of people in the church who can throw their hands in the air and give praise to God just minutes before or soon after being critical, undermining, finding fault and refusing to speak to a specific individual with whom they are angry, and seemingly, never feel guilt or the need to make it right. Something is wrong with this picture. This kind of behavior is offensive to Christ and hurtful to others. It is unfaithfulness to Christ. It is spiritual adultery. It is being unfaithful to the commitment you made to follow Christ and His teachings.

It is like they switch on Christianity, then they switch it off, then back on and then back off, depending on what is going on around them. How can this be? You are good, and then you are bad. I do not get it. This kind of living is not consistent with what the Bible says.

I was discussing this with a friend, and he said that he thinks people pick out the things they are not guilty of and make them sins – adultery, stealing, murder, etc. but the rest they place in an acceptable behavior category. I think he may be right. I do not think God sees it that way.

I have noticed that, *"hatred and fighting, jealousy and anger, constant effort to get the best for yourself, complaints and criticisms, the feeling that everyone else is wrong except those in your own little group"* (Gal 5:19) does more damage to the church than adultery, murder and stealing combined.

No, I am not defending adultery, murder, and stealing, I am trying to emphasize the fact that hatred and fighting, jealously and anger, complaints and criticisms, etc. are major problems that need to be recognized as not acceptable behavior to God and they need to be stopped.

> *2 Corinthians 5:17 (TLB) When someone becomes a Christian, he becomes a brand new person inside. He is not the same anymore. A new life has begun!*

Do not hurry as you read the following. Your own wrong inclinations are from the old person you were before you were born again.

> ➤ *As you read the following verses, just place a little mark of some kind indicating you may need to be reconciled with someone you have wronged in one of the following ways.*

> *Galatians 5:19-26 (TLB) 19 But when you follow your own wrong inclinations, your lives will produce these evil results: impure thoughts, eagerness for lustful pleasure,*
> *20 idolatry, spiritism (that is, encouraging the activity of demons), hatred and fighting, jealousy and anger, constant effort to get the best for yourself, complaints and criticisms, the feeling that everyone else is wrong except those in your own little group — and there will be wrong doctrine,*
> *21 envy, murder, drunkenness, wild parties, and all that sort of*

thing. Let me tell you again, as I have before, that anyone living that sort of life will not inherit the Kingdom of God.

22 But when the Holy Spirit controls our lives he will produce this kind of fruit in us: love, joy, peace, patience, kindness, goodness, faithfulness,

23 gentleness and self-control; and here there is no conflict with Jewish laws.

24 Those who belong to Christ have nailed their natural evil desires to his cross and crucified them there.

25 If we are living now by the Holy Spirit's power, let us follow the Holy Spirit's leading in every part of our lives.

26 Then we will not need to look for honors and popularity, which lead to jealousy and hard feelings.

Ask yourself these questions.

➤ *"Have I tried to make things right between myself and others that I have wronged?"*

➤ *"Have I made any restitution I need to make?"*

➤ *"Have I asked those I have wronged to forgive me or do I justify – rationalize, compare, deny – my wrongs and pretend I did no wrong?"*

The way to renew the relationship, the way to overcome the failures, the way to start over is to remember these three little phrases and use them when needed. *"I was wrong!" "I am sorry!" "Forgive me!"* It is easy to say those words when you do not need to; it is hard when you need to.

The new you will forgive others that have wronged you.

Making things right with others may mean you have to take the lead even when you were not wrong. You may have to choose to forgive those who wronged you in order to be reconciled. I know this may sound strange at first, but try to follow this through with me. I hear people say something like this. "I will forgive them when they come to me and admit they have done me wrong and ask for forgiveness. They are the ones that have done wrong."

You may be right, maybe they were wrong in their mistreatment of you, but that is their burden. That is their responsibility. Your responsibility is to forgive them. You carry the burden when you refuse to forgive. It is hard to forgive people who show no remorse for wrong they have done.

Their responsibility is to seek forgiveness – make restitution, attempt to restore the relationship. They may never do that. If they do not, they will be carrying the burden until they do. They will not have peace until they make things right. The exception might be when they have said no to God so many times that He has turned them loose to their own reprobate mind. They have hardened their heart toward God and no longer feel any guilt or regret for their sinful living. They are living with a false security.

A lady came into my office and told me of the way she was living and said she felt no guilt and wanted to know why. She said she knew in her mind that what she was doing was wrong and not acceptable to God. She had the knowledge, but she had performed this sinful act so many times that she had become hardened. She was blessed when something caused her to question her salvation. Her knowledge of right and wrong caused her to realize she was living in sin and needed to do something about it, even though she felt no sense of guilt or shame any more.

Do you know of someone to which that has happened? That is a very serious and scary thing when one becomes so hardened that they do not hear God calling out to them anymore.

Whether they are even aware of their need to seek forgiveness or not, your responsibility is to forgive them, not make them pay for their wrong, sinful doings. When someone feels the need to make another person pay for their wrongs, they have taken on the role of God.

> Romans 12:19 (TLB) Dear friends, never avenge yourself. Leave that to God, for he has said that he will repay those who deserve it. [Do not take the law into your own hands.]

> Romans 12:19 (Msg) Do not insist on getting even; that's not for you to do. "I'll do the judging," says God. "I'll take care of it."

You are accountable for what you choose to do. Choosing to forgive is a good choice. Let your **_will_** (ability to make a decision) respond to your **_thinking_**, not your **_feeling_** at this point, because that is what God says to do.

Choosing not to forgive is a poor choice. It is an indication that you are allowing your *"imperfect mind"* and *"imperfect emotions"*, not your *"perfectible spirit"* to control your decision.

Even though you are in Christ and Christ is in you, your soul functions still have a job to do. You *think* (your imperfectible mind) about forgiving them. You do not *feel* (your imperfectible emotions) like doing it, but now you are in Christ and Christ is in you because of your spiritual birth. The **SPIRIT** (that is perfectible) steps in and tells you to *"forgive them"*, so you **choose** (your will) to forgive them, in obedience to the spirit of God that lives in you.

Jesus taught his disciples how to pray, and he included forgiveness as a very important part of the prayer.

> *Matthew 6:9-15 (TLB) "Pray along these lines: 'Our Father in heaven, we honor your holy name.*
> *10 We ask that your kingdom will come now. May your will be done here on earth, just as it is in heaven.*
> *11 Give us our food again today, as usual,*
> *12 AND FORGIVE US OUR SINS, JUST AS WE HAVE FORGIVEN THOSE WHO HAVE SINNED AGAINST US.*
> *13 Do not bring us into temptation, but deliver us from the Evil One. Amen.'*
> *14 YOUR HEAVENLY FATHER WILL FORGIVE YOU IF YOU FORGIVE THOSE WHO SIN AGAINST YOU;*
> *15 BUT IF YOU REFUSE TO FORGIVE THEM, HE WILL NOT FORGIVE YOU.*

We cannot honestly say we have forgiven as long as we desire – feel a need – to make people pay or suffer for something they did to us or we perceive they did to us. Our *"imperfectible emotions"* may make suggestions and place thoughts in our *"imperfectible mind"*, that there are ways we can make them pay for what they did. But the *"perfectible spirit"* signals that we should not do that.

That can happen with our mates, our parents, our children, our friends, our co-workers, etc. We may be tempted to do things in an attempt to make them pay for what they did. We may feel (imperfectible emotions) the need to get even by doing or saying something to them or to others about them that hurts them. **Forgiveness _means we will not do that_**. Because we still have our _**imperfectible emotions**_ and our _**imperfectible minds,**_ we are going to have our challenges at times.

Be careful at this point and make sure you do not allow yourself to get caught in the trap of slander and gossiping about their wrongs. The Bible says you are to love them. You are a new person and you can do it.

Remember the "**PADD**" – **P**riorities, **A**ttitude, **D**iscipline and **D**etermination – and use it. You may not like what they are doing or saying. You may be frustrated with their behavior, but as a follower of Christ, you are to want the best for them. That is love. God hates the behavior of some people, but He loves them and wants the best for them.

If it is not a high _**Priority**_ for you to seek and give forgiveness and treat others right even when they do you wrong, something is wrong because that is the way of a born-again Christian – a new person in Christ.

If your _**Attitude**_ is not constantly changing for the better, if you are not exercising your _**Discipline**_ and _**Determination**_ to the best of your abilities, something is wrong with your relationship with Christ. Maybe you are living in a false security. You may think you have something you do not have, spiritually thinking. The Bible clearly teaches that when we become a follower of Christ, we become new people in the way we think and live.

If you are failing repeatedly in these areas of your life – it is a way of life for you – you had better go back and check your born-again credentials. There must be something wrong with them. If you are born again, you have the Holy Spirit of God living in you to help you be a new and different person.

Romans 12:2 (TLB) "Do not copy the behavior and customs of this world, but be a new and different person with a fresh newness in all you do and think. Then you will learn from your own experience how his ways will really satisfy you."

Galatians 5:22(TLB) "But when the Holy Spirit controls our lives he will produce this kind of fruit in us: love, joy, peace, patience, kindness, goodness, faithfulness,
23 gentleness and self-control; and here there is no conflict with Jewish laws.

As long as you live, someone is going to wrong you. People are going to strike out at you. People are going to treat you poorly. It has always been that way and it always will be that way. We must learn to forgive them and move on. This may be the most difficult task you have ever had to do.

Romans 12:21(TLB) "Do not let evil get the upper hand, but conquer evil by doing good."

When the ***imperfect mind and emotions*** do a number on you and pull you in the wrong direction, quickly start doing something good for someone. Do not dwell on the problem.

I was listening to Dr. James Dobson on a talk show and he reminded us that evil people have been around from the beginning of time. He pointed out that much of history has been worse than it is today.

Many people are evil and they will do evil things. They will do things to hurt you intentionally. They will strike out at you when you do not do what they want, when you do not please them, or when things do not go their way. They may lie to you and about you and they may steal from you. They should seek forgiveness, but they may not because they may not be in Christ or have Christ in them. God requires that His children forgive others whether they seek it or not.

Forgiving in your mind, in your heart, and in your spirit is important for you, whether they ask you to forgive them or not. God gave, whether or not people seek what He gave.

John 3:16 (TLB) [16] *For God loved the world so much that he gave his only Son so that anyone who believes in him shall not perish but have eternal life.*

He did His part. Your part is to seek and receive. God has already given forgiveness; people just have to receive what He gave. You have to do it that way also. You forgive those who have wronged you. It is theirs to receive, when they ask. If they do not ask, it is their loss. You have given. You are free. You are clean. You have done all you are required to do. God will withhold His forgiveness if you do not forgive, whether they ask for forgiveness or not.

Matthew 6:14-15 (TLB) [14] *Your heavenly Father will forgive you if you forgive those who sin against you;* [15] *but if you refuse to forgive them, he will not forgive you.*

➤ *Is there someone you need to forgive? Go ahead – forgive him or her and move on with your life.*

Do not be held hostage by their wrongdoing. Once you make the decision to forgive, you are free. You are released. You may still hurt emotionally; you may remember and feel frustration. You may be tempted to pick it up again. ***Those functions are not perfectible***, but ***your spirit is perfectible*** and that is what you must act on. That is the God part in you.

You will not experience the freedom, the good feeling, and relief that is possible, until you develop a spirit of forgiveness based on your need to give it, not on their asking. If you do not forgive others for their wrongs but insist on making them pay by punishing them in some way, you will hurt yourself more than you will hurt them.

> *If they choose not to do what is right, are you going to choose not to do what is right also? Do you want to be wrong just because they have been wrong?*

> *What do you really gain by this?*

> *What do you potentially lose in this life by not forgiving?*

> *What could you lose in the future by not forgiving them?*

Now for the question I suspected some of you had earlier. What if someone does not know he offended you or you do not know you offended him? It is possible that he does not even know he has offended you. There was no intentional wrong done to you, and he is not going to ask forgiveness for something he does not know about. If you wait for him to ask before you forgive, you may carry the load forever and he will be forever free.

The truth may be that he is not as guilty as you think he is. You perceive him to be guilty – so you hold him responsible. Someone may have hurt you, but that may not have been his intention. You may be too sensitive. You may have heard it wrong. You may have interpreted it wrong. Communication is a big issue, and we can communicate poorly and make it sound like something it is not. We can misunderstand. I know those things happen to me. So do not carry a load that is not there. Release it; forgive, whether or not the other person thinks he is guilty of wrongdoing.

Romans 12:21 (TLB) [21] *Don't let evil get the upper hand, but conquer evil by doing good.*

> *Are you going to carry a great load while he goes free?*

Even if your perception is right and he is wrong, it is not your job to hold him responsible for his wrong and sinful living. That belongs to God alone. He decides who is guilty and who is not. He decides who to punish and who not to punish. God alone has perfect knowledge and makes perfect decisions.

When you are offended and do not forgive, you have the burden. You need to forgive, and get rid of it, so you can be free. The person that offended you may be an angry frustrated person who does not intend to seek your forgiveness because he is not sorry for what he has done to you. He may have been rejecting God so long that his heart is calloused – hardened and he does not even feel any guilt.

Forgiveness is a vital part of the present – the now. The sin is in the past, even if it was committed just five minutes ago – it is past and the need for forgiveness is now.

➢ *Whom do you need to forgive?*

It has been my observation through the years that people who admit their failure and seek to right their wrongs – make things right with others – and those who are willing to forgive others are by far happier and less stressed than those who do not. They are not carrying a burden.

Your helper –the Holy Spirit

We are a new person with new connections because we have repented, have been forgiven for our sins, and made a decision to follow the teachings of Christ.

Yet, we are not perfect in:
- Mind – the way we think
- Emotions – the way we feel about issues in life
- Will – the decisions we make.

We need help. We have not become a perfect saint. We are still mere human, and subject to temptation and failure, so we need help from God to be all He wants us to be.

Under no circumstance can we by ourselves, in our imperfectible mind, will, and emotions, ever become the person God wants us to become. We have to have the power of God working in and through our life. This can happen only through the spirit of God working in and through our spirit. When we repented and started following Christ, we opened the door for God to send His spirit into our lives to help us. Before we repented, we could not receive God's spirit; we were not eligible to receive the Holy Spirit of God.

➢ *If you need to, take the time to go back and reread the last chapter. It is important for you to understand the dynamics here.*

I have personally learned that when I am intentionally, purposefully, living as close to all that I know is right – total obedience to the ways of Christ – I do better mentally, emotionally, and make better decisions. My mind, emotions, and will function better. I believe that is because the Holy Spirit has more freedom in my life and more control of my life than when I live on the edge, "dabbling" in the so called "little, insignificant sins".

Practical Word Studies in The New Testament says:

> *…repentance is a turning away from sin and turning toward God. It is a change of mind, a forsaking of sin. It is putting sin out of one's thoughts and behavior. It is resolving never to think or do a thing again. (Cp. Matthew 3:2; Luke 13:2-3; Acts 2:38; Acts 3:19; Acts 8:22; Acts 26:20.) The change is turning away from lying, stealing, cheating, immorality, cursing, drunkenness, and the other so-called glaring sins of the flesh. But the change is also turning away from the silent sins of the spirit such as self-centeredness, selfishness, envy, bitterness, pride, covetousness, anger, evil thoughts, hopelessness, laziness, jealousy, lust.*

Repentance involves two turns. There is a negative turn away from sin and a positive turn toward God. It is a turning to God away from sin, whether sins of thought or action.

We are talking about a complete abandonment of the ways of the past – the "Old Man" – the Satan-controlled man, and becoming a "New Man" in Christ Jesus. I cannot overemphasize this. Just a decision to be a follower of Jesus by saying, "I believe in Jesus" is not enough.

A determination to live a new and different life is required. This is not just a one sided, God-does-everything operation; it involves us also. It cannot happen without our involvement.

When the Holy Spirit lives in us, we are different people. The Holy Spirit cannot live in and control us if we are still "dabbling" in sin. You have read this scripture several times, read it one more time. This thought needs to be imbedded in your mind, so it can surface when needed, to help you make good decisions when you are tempted to do something that would not be pleasing and acceptable to God and in turn, crowd out the Holy Spirit.

Galatians 5:22-26 (TLB) 22 BUT WHEN THE HOLY SPIRIT CONTROLS OUR LIVES he will produce this kind of fruit in us: love, joy, peace, patience, kindness, goodness, faithfulness, 23 gentleness and self-control; and here there is no conflict with Jewish laws.
24 Those who belong to Christ have nailed their natural evil desires to his cross and crucified them there.
25 If we are living now by the Holy Spirit's power, let us follow the Holy Spirit's leading in every part of our lives.

You can live a clean, righteous life with the Holy Spirit's power and you can overcome evil by doing the good the scripture tells us to do.

Romans 12:21 Do not be overcome by evil, but overcome evil with good.

You cannot do it alone; you need the Holy Spirit's power in you. You can have the Holy Spirit's power in you when you are completely committed to honoring God in the way you live at all times. This is the way of a "New Person" in Christ. It is a decision we make – *"... let us follow the Holy spirit's leading in every part of our lives." (Gal 5:25)*. As we follow, he continues to lead. When we quit following, he quits leading. Either we are in control of our lives or we allow God, through His Holy Spirit to be in control of our lives.

One more time, I want to share with you one of my favorite scriptures.

> *Romans 12:1-2 (TLB) 1 And so, dear brothers, I plead with you to give your bodies to God. Let them be a living sacrifice, holy – the kind he can accept. When you think of what he has done for you, is this too much to ask?*
> *2 Do not copy the behavior and customs of this world, but be a new and different person with a fresh newness in all you do and think. Then you will learn from your own experience how his ways will really satisfy you.*

> *Romans 12:2 (NIV) "Do not conform any longer to the pattern of this world, but be transformed by the renewing of your mind. Then you will be able to test and approve what God's will is--his good, pleasing and perfect will."*

The instructions – what **_you_** do:
- Give yourself completely to God;
- Follow His ways completely and fully.

The results:
- True satisfaction
- Long-lasting gratification
- Complete fulfillment
- Pleasure without regrets
- Contentment and happiness

BOTTOM LINE IS YOU GET THE "REAL THING" WHEN YOU DO THE RIGHT THING.

This happens when the Holy Spirit of God works through your spirit. The more you are pleasing to God, the greater and longer lasting your gratification in life will be.

When I was rationalizing and comparing the way I was living – living on the edge, I stumbled and fell too many times. Too often, I became a person I did not want to become. It took me too long to understand that I needed to quit "dabbling" in what is often referred to as "little sins" or "not really a sin". The Practical Word Studies in The New Testament called them the *"... silent sins of the spirit such as self-centeredness, selfishness, envy, bitterness, pride, covetousness, anger, evil thoughts, hopelessness, laziness, jealousy, lust."*

Since I determined I was going to live as close as possible to all I knew was right, life has been much better. There are still some issues, I am still tempted with, and I am not even sure they are sin, but I know I am not comfortable with doing them, so I avoid them, because I would be playing too close to the edge and could eventually end up sinning.

There are some things that others around me do that I do not feel comfortable doing. Sometimes I feel the peer pressure. I just discipline myself and do not do the things that make me feel uncomfortable. That does not mean they are wrong and I am right. I have just reached the place where if it is a question in my mind about whether I should or should not live that way, I do not do it. I do not dabble. I do not test the waters anymore, and life is much better for me than it has ever been. I think I feel the presence of the Holy Spirit in my life more than I ever have. And, you know what? I have reached the place where those issues are not very important to me anymore. I have developed a new **Attitude.**

I use the **PADD** all the time.

- I know what God's **P**riorities are for me, and I have made them my **P**riorities
- I have gotten my **A**ttitude straight – the way I think and feel about God's plan for my life. If that is what He wants, that is what I want; I do not need to discuss it.
- I **D**iscipline myself – I am just making myself do what I know is right regardless of what my human imperfectible mind and emotions are crying out for.
- I am **D**etermined that nothing is going to keep me from doing everything I can humanly do, to do what I know is right. I want to make it to heaven and nothing on this earth is worth missing heaven.

I have had times when I was a mental and emotional wreck and consistently making bad decisions. When I would stop and do a check up on myself, I would almost always be able to recall times when I was playing on the edge - "dabbling", I was not living as close to what I knew was right and pleasing to God as I should have been.

The Bible speaks about a double-minded man being unstable. I am including four translations of this verse to help you really understand what the writer was saying.

James 4:8 (NIV) Come near to God and he will come near to you. Wash your hands, you sinners, and purify your hearts, you double-minded.

James 4:8 (TLB) And when you draw close to God, God will draw close to you. Wash your hands, you sinners, and let your hearts be filled with God alone to make them pure and true to him.

James 4:8 (MSG) Say a quiet yes to God and he'll be there in no time. Quit dabbling in sin. Purify your inner life. Quit playing the field.

James 4:8 (NKJV) Draw near to God and He will draw near to you. Cleanse your hands, you sinners; and purify your hearts, you double-minded.

I am convinced that when we do absolutely everything we know God wants us to do and we do it the way He wants us to do it, He is going to do way more for us via His Holy Spirit helping us with all aspects of life than we could ever imagine.

My pastor - also my brother – often preached a sermon on the subject that I was writing about at the same time I was writing. Thanks little brother.

He just recently preached a great sermon in which he gave us *"Seven dynamic, life changing, facts about the Holy Spirit"*. He gave me permission to use that outline in this material.

God sends His Holy Spirit to <u>convict</u> us of our sin, and the righteousness of God.

John 16:8-12 (NIV) 8 When he comes, he will convict the world of guilt in regard to sin and righteousness and judgment:
9 in regard to sin, because men do not believe in me;
10 in regard to righteousness, because I am going to the Father, where you can see me no longer; 11 and in regard to judgment, because the prince of this world now stands condemned.

God sends His Holy Spirit to <u>guide</u> us to all truth.

John 16:13 But when he, the Spirit of truth, comes, he will guide you into all truth. He will not speak on his own; he will speak only what he hears, and he will tell you what is yet to come.

The Holy Spirit is the best <u>counselor</u> (helper) in the universe.

John 16:7 (NIV) ⁷ But I tell you the truth: It is for your good that I am going away. Unless I go away, the Counselor will not come to you; but if I go, I will send him to you.

The Holy Spirit empowers us to be <u>witnesses</u>.

Acts 1:8 (TLB) ⁸ But when the Holy Spirit has come upon you, you will receive power to testify about me with great effect, to the people in Jerusalem, throughout Judea, in Samaria, and to the ends of the earth, about my death and resurrection."

The Holy Spirit makes an impact on how we live.

Galatians 5:16, 22,23 (NIV) [16] *So I say, live by the Spirit, and you will not gratify the desires of the sinful nature.* [22] *But the fruit of the Spirit is love, joy, peace, patience, kindness, goodness, faithfulness,* [23] *gentleness and self-control. Against such things there is no law.*

The Holy Spirit will guide us with the right words to say.

Luke 12:12 (NIV) [12] *for the Holy Spirit will teach you at that time what you should say."*

The Holy Spirit is a gift from God for the asking.

Luke 11:13 (NIV) [13] *If you then, though you are evil, know how to give good gifts to your children, how much more will your Father in heaven give the Holy Spirit to those who ask him!"*

When you repent and start following the ways of Christ, you do not walk alone, God walks with you, through His Holy Spirit working in and through your spirit. A transformation has taken place in you! You are a new person. Live like it.

**YOU ARE GOING TO CHANGE
THE WAY YOU LIVE
BY CHANGING THE WAY YOU THINK.**

**THIS HAPPENS WHEN YOUR PRIORITIES
AND YOUR ATTITUDE ARE IN SYNC WITH
GOD.**

**THIS HAPPENS WHEN HIS HOLY SPIRIT
WORKS IN AND THROUGH YOUR SPIRIT –
THE ONLY PART OF YOU THAT IS
PERFECTIBLE.**

LEARN TO LIVE BY THE "PADD"

PRIORITIES

ATTITUDE

DISCIPLINE

DETERMINATION.

THREE

OBSTACLES AND FALSE POSITIVES

Stumbling

Stumbling is something that most of us have experienced physically and spiritually. I hate stumbling. I do it going up or down the steps in my house. I especially hate stumbling when I am in public where people see me. I certainly never stumble on purpose. Usually when we stumble in public, we look around to see if anyone saw us. We hope no one saw us. I have stumbled spiritually more times than I want to remember. I hope not many people noticed.

I do not stumble spiritually on purpose either, but I do it and I have to deal with it. I cannot ignore it. I cannot pretend everything is OK when it is not. I cannot pretend it did not happen and just move on in life.

You, most likely are going to stumble and fall spiritually. You are going to fail at some point in your spiritual walk. Almost everybody I have visited with about this issue admits to falling at some point. Living the Christian life is hard, but stumbling and falling does not have to be the end. You get up, seek God's forgiveness, and move on. Some people have a problem with admitting they stumbled and fell, and asking forgiveness, so they rationalize and excuse it, or deny it, and pretend it did not happen. That does not fix anything.

Some will say, "I don't have to seek forgiveness for stumbling and falling because it wasn't intentional, and because I didn't intend to stumble and fall, grace will take care of it. I think those who have a hard time admitting they stumbled and fell and cannot say they are sorry and seek forgiveness, regardless of the circumstances, may have a pride problem, which can be a sin. Maybe they need to deal with their pride issue. We will cover that in the next section.

We are not talking about someone that just deliberately, intentionally, knowingly, on purpose, made a decision to go against God's will and plan for his or her life. That is not stumbling and falling, that is outright willful sin against God – that is rebellion. They just jumped off the edge of Niagara Falls on purpose, because they wanted to. They did not get too close to the edge, stumble, and fall.

I believe there are two ways to stumble... to fail... to fall.

1. A mistake is one way, something that happened and there was no way to avoid it. We were blindsided. I believe grace will cover that even if we happen to die in the process of our falling. I would call this a true mistake. The heart/spirit was right, the mind for some reason failed. A wrong happened but it had nothing to do with a heart condition, it was honestly the result of our imperfect mind and or emotions and will. The human in us failed, but our heart was right. I think it is possible to fail/fall and not even be aware of our failure to do what we should have done.

2. Stumbling because we were careless is a second way, taking a risk we should not have taken. We did not take the precautions we should have taken to avoid the fall. We pushed the envelope. We did or did not do, as we knew we should or should not do; and therefore set ourselves up for

the fall. I believe we are responsible for that and need to confess our failure and seek forgiveness!

Let me illustrate.

I do not think anybody intends to have a head-on wreck and end up in a wheelchair for the rest of his or her life. They passed on a curve thinking they could see far enough ahead to see if there was a car coming. They took a risk that they should not have taken. They are responsible for their personal injuries and the injuries of others. The consequences do not change just because there was no intention to have a wreck. The driver is responsible for his reckless, risky driving and has to pay the price.

A cute blonde makes a pass at you and you choose to entertain it, believing in your mind that you are strong enough spiritually to avoid going too far. You should have ignored it and walked in the opposite direction, but you did not because you were experiencing some immediate gratification in the attention she was giving you.

In all the years of counseling, I never heard anyone admit he or she intended to have an affair. In every case, people put themselves in a situation that made it easy for an affair to happen even though they did not intend for it to happen. They are responsible for the consequences because they consciously made poor choices.

When I go to a bank and make a loan for a new vehicle, I am accepting responsibility for the payments. If I should, at an emotional moment, purchase a new television for $650 and then find myself unable to make the car payment, the banker does not say, "Oh well, we all make mistakes once in a while. It is Ok. I will cover it for you this month." The banker does not have the responsibility of taking care of our payment just because we were reckless in our spending.

However it happens, it happens. We cannot just ignore it and try to move on as if it did not happen. Regardless of how it happened, it is the responsibility of Christians to help each other up when they fall. If a fellow Christian falls, you be one of the first to lift him up, encourage him to repent and continue in his walk with Christ.

YOU DO NOT GO TALK TO OTHERS ABOUT IT.

The Bible tells us that some will stumble and fall and we are to help restore them by giving forgiveness and encouraging them to seek forgiveness from God. Do that for yourself. Pick yourself up, seek God's forgiveness, be restored in your relationship with God, forgive yourself, and move on.

Allow someone else to help you get back up. Do not be too proud to go to a friend and share your failure and ask them to help you get back on the right path.

If you do fall into sin and another person begins to criticize you, slander, and gossip about you or avoid you, do not let that discourage you. Do not try to defend yourself, just work on getting your life straightened out and leave that individual to God. That person needs love and understanding, too. He has fallen into sin himself and someone needs to help him find his way back to the right path. Becoming involved in some kind of a conflict with him will not help you or him, so just work on your problem and leave him alone, at least till you get your own spiritual life headed in the right direction.

SATAN WOULD LOVE TO GET YOU SIDETRACKED BY LOOKING AT SOMEONE ELSE'S PROBLEM AND FAIL TO DEAL WITH YOUR OWN.

If he can, Satan will try to get you to *"compare"* your failure to someone else's failure and *"rationalize"* (two of Satan's defense attorneys coming to your defense) that you are Ok because your failure was not as big and bad as his failure.

Some of your greatest stumbling blocks may come from people who called themselves Christians. Do not let that alarm you. Look past them, and move on. In another section, we will deal with the problem of judging. For now, just do not let someone's judgmental attitude and critical words discourage you and stop you from dealing with your failure.

I am certain, that at some point I have caused others to stumble. We need to be careful so we do not cause others to stumble by what we do or say. Sometimes we cause others to stumble when we do not realize it. When we realize we caused someone to stumble, we should do whatever we have to do to correct that.

> Galatians 6:1-2 (TLB) "Dear brothers, if a Christian is overcome by some sin, you who are godly should gently and humbly help him back onto the right path, remembering that next time it might be one of you who is in the wrong. ² Share each other's troubles and problems, and so obey our Lord's command."

> Galatians 6:1 (MSG) "Live creatively, friends. If someone falls into sin, forgivingly restore him, saving your critical comments for yourself. You might be needing forgiveness before the day's out."

There will most likely be times when others need you to help them back up. Be there for them.

The pride issue

Do you have a pride problem; you just cannot bring yourself to the place where you can say, "I was wrong. I am wrong. I sinned. I am a sinner, and I need help. Forgive me!" You can talk about all the good things you do, all the prayers you say, all the scriptures you can quote, all the people you have helped, your faithfulness in going to church, etc. but you can't say, "I am sorry. I failed. Forgive me".

I searched "pride" on my computer Bible program and it gave me 6,313 results. I started reading through them. I read from several different translations or versions and from several different commentaries and other Bible study books. Only a few times did I find pride used in a positive situation. Pride can be a good thing or it can be a very destructive thing. For the most part, it is destructive.

Psalm 10:4 (NIV) "In his pride the wicked does not seek him; in all his thoughts there is no room for God."

**DO NOT BE TOO PROUD TO SAY, "I AM SO SORRY, PLEASE FORGIVE ME",
AND MOVE ON.**

Proverbs 8:13 (NLT) All who fear the LORD will hate evil. Therefore, I hate pride and arrogance, corruption and perverse speech.

Proverbs 11:2 (NIV) When pride comes, then comes disgrace, but with humility comes wisdom.

Proverbs 13:10 (NIV) Pride only breeds quarrels, but wisdom is found in those who take advice.

Proverbs 29:23 (TLB) Pride ends in a fall, while humility brings honor.

Some people just cannot come to the place where they can say, "Hey, I was wrong. I am sorry. Forgive me." They have too much pride.

If it is hard for you to admit to a friend or a family member that you were wrong, that you failed, that you messed up, it is probably hard for you to tell God that you were wrong when you committed a sin. You would rather call them mistakes, errors, or just brush it off by saying:

- "I'm just human".
- "It wasn't that bad".
- "Nobody is perfect".
- "Everybody fails at some point".

When I was doing pre-marital counseling, I tried to drive home the thought that there would be problems in almost all, if not all, marriages. I told them the question was not if they would do something that hurt each other; it was when and how often. I told them that both of them would be wrong at times. I also told them that it would be easy to defend and excuse their own misbehavior and be critical of their mate when they were wrong. I tried to get them to remember this little phrase.

BEING WRONG – FAILING – IS NOT BAD.
BEING TOO PROUD TO ADMIT YOUR FAILURE
AND CORRECT IT, IS BAD!

I told them the way to renew the relationship, the way to overcome the failures, the way to start over, is to remember these four little phrases and use them when needed.

- "I was wrong!"
- "I am sorry!"
- "Forgive me!"

- "I love you!"

Then you do everything in your power to prove your love by not doing again those things that created the stress, the anger, the frustration, the resentment, the chasm between you. Saying you are sorry means little or nothing if you just keep doing the same things over and over and do not make any attempt to change.

It is rare to find someone that doesn't have a hard time saying, "I failed," "I was wrong," "I am sorry," "forgive me," when they fail, regardless of how serious the failure was. It is easy to say those words when we do not need to say them; but when we need to say them, it is hard. It seems like an unbreakable chain of pride binds us. I think it is something we have to force ourselves to do because we know it is the right thing to do.

Do not forget to use the _PADD_ – _P_riorities, _A_ttitude, _D_iscipline, and _D_etermination. Satan will come on with all the forces he can to keep you from saying to God, "I have sinned, I am sorry, forgive me, I love you and I will serve you".

It is crucial that you understand the importance of admitting failure, seeking forgiveness, and correcting the failure. This must be high on your Priority list. This is something you have to do. Develop an Attitude that says, it is Ok to fail. That does not mean you are a terrible person; it means you are human. It is not OK to rationalize, deny, compare, or ignore the failure. You just need to Discipline yourself – make yourself, force yourself -- to do what you know you need to do.

Become so Determined, so strong-minded, so resolute that you are going to do what is right that you just do it regardless of how you feel. Do not postpone it and say you will do it later. That too often becomes a permanent escape from doing what you need to do.

Once you break that chain of pride, you can do it more easily and quickly the next time. Finally, it becomes a way of life for you when you know you are wrong, to say, "Hey, I was wrong and I am sorry; please forgive me!"

I know how this works because I have been down this route. Being able to say, "Hey, I was wrong and I am sorry; please forgive me!" needs to become a way of life for us because we are going to fail more than just once. We do it because we are sorry and we wish we had not done whatever we did that was wrong. It is a heart issue, not just a moving of the lips. The words are an expression of our regret that we sinned or failed in some way. We train ourselves to recognize our failure and immediately attempt to correct it. We do it not because we feel like it; we do it because it is the right thing to do. With our imperfectible minds and emotions, we will always have an opportunity to learn this skill.

> *Do you have a pride issue that keeps you from saying that you are sorry and want forgiveness, either from God, or others?*

> *How are you going to deal with this? Exactly what are you going to do to develop this attitude in your life?*

It will get easier when you realize how much more free you feel, how much peace you have when you do it with a genuine attitude of repentance – making things right with God and others.

I can remember well the day – I was in college – I first broke the chain of pride and said it to a friend after we had argued bitterly over an unimportant issue. I was wrong and I knew it, but something inside me prohibited me from admitting my wrong. I struggled and struggled, I made accusations, I raised my voice, I made threats and finally (I think the Holy Spirit of God prompted me and helped me) I broke and said, "Bob, (not his name) you are right and I am wrong, I am sorry; please forgive me."

The battle was over. I felt such peace. I was so relieved. I felt so good. I was free. I was a new person. I was not angry with my friend any longer. The enemy had been defeated, and we became much better friends. I have had to repeat that process many times over the years and it always feels good, even though it is not always easy. Often, when I need to do it again, I have a flashback to how good it felt when I, for the first time, reconciled and made things right with someone by saying, "I am wrong; I am sorry; forgive me".

Pride has created tons of unnecessary problems for people through the years. It has put people in mental and emotional prisons. It has created gigantic periods of grief and guilt that they did not have to live with.

The results of pride can be:
- Broken marriages
- Divided families
- Lost jobs
- Divided churches
- Missing heaven
- And more

➢ *What is your pride doing to you?*

➢ *Where is it keeping you from being all God wants you to be?*

> *What are you losing by being too proud to admit you have a problem?*

> *What is your pride costing you in the way of relationships?*

> *Where do you have a pride problem that you need to work on resolving?*

We learned earlier that giving forgiveness brings relief; it gives freedom and allows you to move on. The same is true with pride when we confess our wrongs. We are no longer burdened with the load. We no longer drag around chains of conflict fueled by anger, bitterness, and resentment. We find relief by breaking our pride, confessing our wrongs, and admitting our need for forgiveness and starting over.

**TAKE THE PRIVILEGE OF A NEW BEGINNING.
RECONCILE AND START OVER.**

**REMEMBER, IT IS NOT BAD
TO BE WRONG, TO FAIL.**

**IT IS BAD WHEN YOU ARE TOO
PROUD TO ADMIT YOUR FAILURE
AND START OVER.**

This is the way it works, "We win by losing." Until one has reached the place where he is able to say, "I failed… I sinned… I did wrong and I am sorry… forgive me" he will never have the relationship with God or others that he could have. He cheats himself out of the better life.

Whether it is your relationship with your mate, your child, your parent, your neighbor or God, you can fix the problem. You can mend the relationship by acknowledging your wrong, confessing your sorrow, seeking forgiveness, and then changing.

YOU BREAK THE PRIDE AND WIN!

Do you remember when your mom used to say, "Tell your brother you are sorry?" You did, but you did not mean it. You just did not want to reap the consequences if you did not do as your mother told you to do. With God, if you do not mean it, you are in big trouble because He can read your mind and see your heart. He knows everything. He sees inside you.

You may not feel sorrowful, sad – in an emotional sense – but you intellectually understand you have been offending God and you regret that. You are sorry that you offended God. Then you say, "I am sorry... I sinned... I failed... I was wrong... forgive me". Use whatever terms you want to use, but you have to let the pride be broken and ask God for help. Asking for help is admitting you cannot do it by yourself.

BREAKING THE PRIDE AND ADMITTING
YOU NEED HELP IS A BOLD AND PRODUCTIVE STEP.

TAKE IT!

Judging – a judgmental attitude

I am not talking about being a judge at a music festival and casting my vote on who is the best.

I am not talking about observing the way a person lives and comparing it with the ways the Bible tells us to live. That is an observation – it is comparing one's behavior – his deeds, to the laws of God telling us how we should or should not be living. In reality, it is a warning, a red flag. We should, in love, throw up red flags when we see someone we love and care about, living in a way that is not acceptable and pleasing to God.

Think of me riding with you as you speed through a school zone at 60MPH, and I say, "Hey man, you are driving way too fast! We are in a school zone. You may kill a kid." I am just stating the facts. I am warning you. I am not judging. I do not have a judgmental attitude that is taking aim at you because you are not measuring up to how I think you should be driving.

I am talking about a judgmental spirit, attitude, and mouth that is critical, condemning and destructive. Some people observe every little thing others say, and/or do. Then they make a judgmental statement about issues that are none of their business and have nothing to do with righteousness or wickedness, according to the word of God. They are not trying to warn them and help them. They seem to think God has appointed them to take care of the issues in life that God is missing. My father used to have a saying that I try to remember when I see or hear something that I do not understand or like and am tempted to say something I should not say. He would say, "I guess that is really none of our concern, is it!"

There will always be people around to find fault, criticize, and judge you when it is really none of their concern. One who has a judgmental spirit and attitude can damage relationships and cause people to get discouraged.

A woman in the church where I was the Pastor must have thought she was assigned by God to keep the pastor humble and straight. She did it in board meetings and outside board meetings. She was constantly making judgmental, critical statements to me and about me to others. I was the country bumpkin who knew nothing and was obviously not following the leading of God as pastor. It was a very discouraging situation. It kept me beat down and defensive.

It was becoming a spiritual problem for me because of the attitude that I was developing. One day she came to me and told me that she did not like the way I was handling a specific situation. She told me that God told her to tell me that I needed to change the way I was handling this situation. I told her to tell God He needed to come directly to me because I was stubborn and would not listen to her any longer.

Honestly, I was grateful when she and her husband left the church because she was a great discouragement to many others also. She was a stumbling block. She sat in judgment on me constantly. I was always doing something wrong, doing something she thought I should not be doing, or not doing what she thought I should be doing. In short, I was a failing pastor in her judgment.

Life will always provide someone who feels the need to sit in judgment on what you are saying or what you are doing. Do not allow that person to discourage you.

Do not get lost in your walk with God. Put your eyes on God's ways and follow what you know is right. Pray for the one that wants to play God in your life. Do not respond in a critical way; do not fight back!

I wish I could say I have always done that. I have not. My biggest regrets, my greatest sorrows, my worst hurts, as I look back are not what happened to me, but how I handled it. I wish life had an "undo" button.

There are people in my life that I now avoid because I know that most likely if I am in a conversation with them they are going to find something about me that is wrong, they are going to correct what I say and what I do. I used to argue and fuss with them, now I avoid them. I am kind, I speak and smile, I treat them well, but we do not spend much time together.

We need to be careful how we respond to others. We may need to be more lenient, show more grace, and be more considerate. We need to understand that there may be something we don't' know, rather than start judging and making accusations.

Luke 6:37-42 (NIV) 37 "Do not judge, and you will not be judged. Do not condemn, and you will not be condemned. Forgive, and you will be forgiven.

38 Give, and it will be given to you. A good measure, pressed down, shaken together and running over, will be poured into your lap. For with the measure you use, it will be measured to you."

39 He also told them this parable: "Can a blind man lead a blind man? Will they not both fall into a pit?

40 A student is not above his teacher, but everyone who is fully trained will be like his teacher.

41 "Why do you look at the speck of sawdust in your brother's eye and pay no attention to the plank in your own eye?

42 How can you say to your brother, 'Brother, let me take the speck out of your eye,' when you yourself fail to see the plank in your own eye? You hypocrite, first take the plank out of your eye, and then you will see clearly to remove the speck from your brother's eye.

Failing to forgive and forget

We are talking about obstacles that may cause us to stumble in our Christian walk. Some people remember some of their own past and become discouraged and fearful that someone else may know about it and judge them by their past instead of what and who they are now as a new person in Christ.

It is so easy to look back and see things that were not as they should have been. We all have those times that we wish were not in our personal history books. We would like to hit the delete button, but there is no delete button to push and we are tortured by our past.

It is important to remember that if God has forgiven us, it is as if it never happened. God does not remember the things He has forgiven. Remember that and focus on this thought: God has forgiven me, so I will forgive myself also, and try to forget it. When it does come to your mind, remind yourself that God has forgiven you and forgotten it.

I have a few items in my past that sometimes haunt me in a big way and I have to tell myself that is the past – that was me then and I am what I am now and I know I am acceptable and pleasing to God now and that is all that counts. If others know and have a need to spread the bad news about my past, in the end they have to deal with God for their behavior: judging, undermining, gossiping, slandering, etc.

Some people feel the need to remind us of our regretful past, or the past of others. It is discouraging and frustrating. It creates unnecessary fear and defensiveness and causes division. One reason I can think of for their doing that is that they are dealing with their own regrettable past and it makes them feel better if they can talk about how bad somebody else was. Another reason I can think of is that they want to hurt that person. That is gossip, slander, backbiting, undermining, etc., and it is a sin.

Do not let the forgiven past become a stumbling block. Remember to forgive and forget. I know you cannot actually erase from your memory some of the past, but you do not have to be rehearsing it all the time. When your past haunts you, start praising the Lord for all your blessings, focus on the good, and do something good for someone else. You will be amazed how much better you feel about yourself, when you have completed doing something good for someone else.

(Just throwing it in again as a reminder.)

Romans 12:21 Do not be overcome by evil, but overcome evil with good.

Notice in the following scripture, we are to focus on the true and good and right. Something may be true in the sense that it did happen, but not good and right. Focus on the **_true and good and right - praiseworthy_**. Then, the peace of God will be with you.

Philippians 4:8-9 (TLB) [8] And now, brothers, as I close this letter, let me say this one more thing: Fix your thoughts on what is true and good and right. Think about things that are pure and lovely, and dwell on the fine, good things in others. Think about all you can praise God for and be glad about.
9 Keep putting into practice all you learned from me and saw me doing, and the God of peace will be with you.

Philippians 4:8-9 (NKJV) [8] *Finally, brethren, whatever things are true, whatever things are noble, whatever things are just, whatever things are pure, whatever things are lovely, whatever things are of good report, if there is any virtue and if there is anything praiseworthy--meditate on these things.*
[9] *The things which you learned and received and heard and saw in me, these do, and the God of peace will be with you.*

Praying

Praying can be a false positive. A false positive is something that looks and sounds good, but in reality, it is not. Sometimes people do certain things because that is what they are supposed to do. They do it out of habit, it becomes a ritual, and there is no sincerity in it. I think praying is one of those things we can do as a habit or ritual that has little or no meaning. Some people can get very wordy and go on and on with very impressive dissertations in their prayer. Sorry! Praying is not enough. You may have voiced certain words and phrases. You may have prayed and gone through certain religious rituals, and have never really repented. Praying (saying words) alone can be dangerous. It can give you a false security. You can think everything is OK because you pray.

I was having coffee with a friend a few years ago and he said something about the "great prayer" that someone prayed. Then he said, "I think he is really spiritual, you can tell how spiritual someone is by their prayer". That is not what the Bible says.

Listen to what Jesus said about great public prayers.

Matthew 6:5 (NIV) [5] *"And when you pray, do not be like the hypocrites, for they love to pray standing in the synagogues and on the street corners to be seen by men. I tell you the truth, they have received their reward in full.*

Matthew 6:5 (MSG) [5] *"And when you come before God, don't turn that into a theatrical production either. All these people making a regular show out of their prayers, hoping for stardom! Do you think God sits in a box seat?*

You may be able to verbalize some very impressive prayers and you may pray a lot about many different issues and approach God about everything you do, but if you have not really repented, you haven't met the requirements for heaven. Your praying – saying words – may be a false positive.

Recently I was trying to help an individual find his way through a deep, dark, troubling time. The problem was bigger than we were. Human effort was not going to fix the problem. There was no way we were going to sit down and work this problem out on paper or talk enough to fix the problem. We needed some real miracle-working power from God. I knew we were going to need God's love, forgiveness, patience, and power to work through this. We needed God to be the key player. We needed Him, and we needed His input. We needed Him on our team.

I decided the best place to start was to ask this individual about his relationship with God. I did not really know him and I wanted to know about his spiritual life. I wanted him to see, recognize his true relationship with God. What did he know and believe about God? How did he see God? Did he even believe in God? Did he have knowledge about what is morally right and wrong? Did he know what the Bible says about how he should be living? Was he being obedient to what he knows the Bible says about how he should be living? I asked him to tell me about his knowledge of and relationship with God.

The first move from darkness to light is from *"not knowing to knowing"*. The second move from darkness to light is from *"not doing to doing"*. I was almost certain from what I had already heard that he did not know and certainly was not doing what was right and pleasing to God.

His immediate reply was that he prayed all the time. "I pray several times a day", he told me. I asked again, this time I asked specifically if he knew Christ as his Savior. His reply was something like, "I pray a lot about my problem." I asked the question in different ways, several times, if he had repented and turned to follow Christ. I asked if he had confessed his sins and asked for forgiveness. His reply was usually the same. "I pray all the time," or "I have prayed about this problem a lot." "I always pray." "Of course I pray."

In our lengthy meeting, I concluded that he did not believe that the way he lived was important, as long as he believed there was a God, and he prayed to God. He seemed to believe that God was just sitting up there somewhere waiting for people to ask for things, and He (God) would grant the request. He could not understand why God was not responding.

Praying without a relationship with God (except when trying to start a relationship via a prayer of repentance) is like seeing a banker on the street, and asking for a loan. You know he is a banker, but you don't really know him and have never done any business with his bank, yet, you think you can just walk up to him and ask for a loan.

I was determined to get the answer I wanted and needed. I do not remember the exact content of the conversation, but it went something like this. "Do you know Jesus Christ as your personal Savior, that is, have you ever come to the place where you knew you were a sinner and had no hope of going to heaven unless you repented and turned to Jesus, seeking forgiveness for your sinful ways?" His answer was, "I guess I never knew I had to do that."

Just praying – saying words, talking – about things in this life is not enough. You cannot be born again and experience the spiritual birth until you repent. You cannot call upon God expecting Him to answer your request unless you have a relationship with Him that warrants your asking Him for something.

First, pray for forgiveness, develop a relationship, and then ask for favors. Saying a lot of words and calling it prayer can be a false positive – it sounds good, it looks good, but has no value.

Reading the Bible, quoting scripture, and praising the Lord

This can be another example of a false positive. Anybody can read the Bible, quote scripture, throw their hands in the air and give praise to God, and still live in sin daily. If someone believes that God exists and also believes that Jesus is God's son, but does what he feels like doing instead of what God has told him to do may have a false positive. Someone may think believing God exists, going through religious rituals, and saying, "Praise the Lord" will give them the promise of heaven, but it will not.

I wanted to title this book, CHOOSING HEAVEN – MORE THAN, SAYING A PRAYER, BELIEVING IN GOD, BELIEVING IN JESUS, GOING TO CHURCH, SINGING IN THE CHOIR, SERVING ON THE CHURCH BOARD, GIVING TO THE POOR AND NEEDY, BEING NICE, DOING GOOD, READING THE BIBLE, ETC. HAVE YOU GOT TIIE PICTURE?

Believing in Christ, repenting of our sins, and obeying God's instructions for living, will make one ready for heaven. Knowledge does not make one ready for heaven. Salvation, redemption, forgiveness of our sins, and avoiding hell is a result of repentance followed by obedience.

Hebrews 5:9 (NIV) 9 and, once made perfect, he became the source of eternal salvation for all who obey him

Hebrews 5:9 (TLB) 9 It was after he had proved himself perfect in this experience that Jesus became the Giver of eternal salvation to all those who obey him.

Hebrews 5:9 (NKJV) 9 And having been perfected, He became the author of eternal salvation to all who obey Him,

Doing good things

Joining the church, serving on the church board, singing in the choir, giving to missions, tithing, visiting the sick, giving to the poor, etc., does not make you a Christian and qualify you for heaven. These are good, positive, wonderful, magnificent things to do, but they do not prepare you for heaven. If you think doing these positive things will take you to heaven, they will not. They are false positives.

Carrying an "I'm not really all that bad" attitude

This type of thinking – this attitude – can be another false positive. It is easy to excuse your sins by rationalizing that you do not do **"really bad"** things. It is equally easy after you have repented and started following Christ, to fall back into doing those things you did as a sinner and rationalize that they aren't **"that big of a deal"**, or not all **"that bad"**.

What do you mean when you say you are not all "that bad"? How bad is "that bad?" Are you a sinner and stand in need of forgiveness only if you reach level six out of a possible ten? That puts you over the halfway mark. You need to repent and ask God for forgiveness for any and all sins. You do not have to be "really bad" to need to repent.

Maybe you think you have committed only what the world considers *"small sins"* that are not *"**that bad**"* and you do not really need to do anything about them because they are so small. When I was pastoring I went to the hospital to see one of our high school football players. He was big and strong, but he was injured. His knee was messed up pretty bad. He was getting ready to go into surgery. We visited for a while and then I said, "Mike, can I pray for you before you go into surgery?" He looked totally shocked and replied, "Is it that serious?"

➢ *Are you still thinking there are sizes of the sin? You need to get your mind straightened out on that issue. There are sins, not "big sins" and "little sins".*

There are acts of sin that are bigger than other acts of sin. For instance, murder is a much more serious act of sin with greater consequences in society than lying on your income tax return about how much you gave to the church last year. However, they are both sins.

Romans 3:23 (TLB) 23 Yes, all have sinned; all fall short of God's glorious ideal;
24 yet now God declares us "not guilty" of offending him if we trust in Jesus Christ, who in his kindness freely takes away our sins.

1 John 1:8-10 (MSG) 8 If we claim that we're free of sin, we're only fooling ourselves. A claim like that is errant nonsense.

9 On the other hand, if we admit our sins – make a clean breast of them – he will not let us down; he'll be true to himself. He'll forgive our sins and purge us of all wrongdoing.

10 If we claim that we've never sinned, we out-and-out contradict God – make a liar out of him. A claim like that only shows off our ignorance of God.

1 John 1:8-10 (TLB) 8 If we say that we have no sin, we are only fooling ourselves and refusing to accept the truth.

9 But if we confess our sins to him, he can be depended on to forgive us and to cleanse us from every wrong. And it is perfectly proper for God to do this for us because Christ died to wash away our sins.

10 If we claim we have not sinned, we are lying and calling God a liar, for he says we have sinned.

This is the way it is.

- You are a sinner if you have not repented – confessed your sins to Christ and turned away from the sinful way you once lived.
- Sinners do not go to heaven. I am not talking about forgiven sinners; I am referring to active sinners, those that keep on sinning.
- It does not make any difference if you have stolen an apple or a sack full of apples or hijacked a truckload of apples, you have stolen, and stealing is a sin. Unfortunately, the Bible does not differentiate between how much or how little you steal.
- The Bible does not say you can take God's name in vain twenty times before you are a sinner. It says do not take God's name in vain.
- The Bible does not say a lie is sinful only if the earthly consequences are severe.
- It does not say you can commit adultery as long as nobody finds out about it and nobody is hurt.
- You do not have to be a bad, mean, angry, lying thief that just committed adultery or robbed a bank to be a sinner. You just have to be disobedient to the teachings of God. You just

have to say, "No thank you God; I think I will just do it my way!"

- The only way to become an ex-active sinner – a sinner saved by grace – is to repent, confess your belief in Jesus Christ, admit your sinful condition. Yes, to get forgiveness you have to admit you are a sinner regardless of the size of the act of sin, and you have to seek forgiveness.
- The only way to continue in your relationship with God, is to seek His forgiveness each time you sin, even if in your mind it is only a "little" sin. In God's mind, it is just sin.

➤ *Do you try to excuse your sinful behavior by saying, "I'm not that bad" or "it's not that big of a deal"? Think about this before you answer. Do not just pass it by because you do not want to deal with it.*

➤ *List the issues that you have a tendency to downplay to keep from feeling guilty or because you do not want to make some changes.*

LEARN TO LIVE BY THE "PADD"

PRIORITIES

ATTITUDE

DISCIPLINE

DETERMINATION.

FOUR
PULLING IT ALL TOGETHER

This book summed up in one chapter.

- This is what you do.
- This is what you get.
- This is how you do it.

This is what you do

Repent and be born again

A sinner cannot just jump into a relationship with God with an attitude that says, "Hey God, I want to be on your side. I like the idea of heaven. Here I am, let's celebrate." He has to approach God with a repentant, "I am sorry" attitude of the heart, possibly sorrowful in the emotional sense, but not necessarily.

John 3:3 (TLB) Jesus said, "With all the earnestness I possess I tell you this: Unless you are born again, you can never get into the Kingdom of God."

Luke 13:3 (NIV) "I tell you, no! But unless you repent, you too will all perish."

Luke 13:3 (TLB) "Not at all! And don't you realize that you also will perish unless you leave your evil ways and turn to God?"

Luke 15:7 (NIV) "I tell you that in the same way there will be more rejoicing in heaven over one sinner who repents than over ninety-nine righteous persons who do not need to repent."

Luke 15:10 (NIV) "In the same way, I tell you, there is rejoicing in the presence of the angels of God over one sinner who repents."

Acts 2:38 (NIV) "Peter replied, "Repent and be baptized, every one of you, in the name of Jesus Christ for the forgiveness of your sins. And you will receive the gift of the Holy Spirit."

Acts 3:19 (NIV) "Repent, then, and turn to God, so that your sins may be wiped out, that times of refreshing may come from the Lord,"

Acts 3:19 (TLB) "Now change your mind and attitude to God and turn to him so he can cleanse away your sins and send you wonderful times of refreshment from the presence of the Lord "

Acts 26:20 (NIV) "...I preached that they should repent and turn to God and prove their repentance by their deeds."

> **Have you just been religious, or have you really repented and turned from your sin?**

There must definitely be a sense of remorse with an apologetic attitude about your sinful past. Some can be sorry for what they have done because they simply recognize their wrong, and they want to correct it, but they never get emotional about it. They are not emotional people. It is not an emotional issue; it is a spiritual – inner being – heart issue.

Repentance is the starting point. I want to be careful here. I am just putting out the caution flag. I think the "sinner's prayer" that Christianity has adopted may give some people a false security. Do not go away and say you read in this book that the sinner's prayer does not work. I am not saying that. I think the motive is right and I think it can and does work. However, I think it is possible to see it as a shortcut that does not work. It is not like the "get out of jail free" cards we got when we played Monopoly.

Listen carefully to what I am saying. I think it can create a problem. Please notice I said, "can" not "does." Work through this with me. The intent of the "sinner's prayer" is to encourage people to make a decision to receive Christ – to become a Christian. That is good. We just need to make sure people understand what true repentance means before we have them say a few words, believing this will give them a ticket to heaven.

Some people know little or nothing about becoming a Christian. They have never heard anything about repentance and the born again life. They know nothing about what the Bible teaches concerning a new life and turning away from sin. Just repeating a few words that mean nothing to them, can give them a false security. It may allow one to say words without any understanding or conviction that they have done anything wrong and need forgiveness.

They may not have the slightest idea that they are going to have to make some changes in the way they live. If they understand what it means to be a Christian and they know what is required to become a Christian, then at any point in their life they decide to become a Christian, the sinner's prayer will do the job. They have all the knowledge they need; they just need to make a decision to do something about what they know.

Some people have no regret for the way they have offended God with their unacceptable behavior (sins) and have no desire to change. They just decided that heaven sounds like a great deal, and if saying those words is all they have to do, to get there, why not do it. It is like a free meal – do not ask any questions, just eat.

That can turn into a counterfeit salvation. They can say words with their mouth, without anything taking place in the spiritual part of their being, their heart. Their way of thinking has not changed which means there will be no change in the way they live.

It is the heart, not the words

A friend of mine, Robin Barnhart, said,

"I think the sinner's prayer is much like saying wedding vows to your spouse. Your heart has to honestly be His in order for it to mean anything, just like words said as your vows do not mean anything if you are truly not whole-heartedly invested in loving that person. It is all dependent on the investment of your heart."

There was a man with an illness for which there was no cure. He was certain to die, but he did not know that. The doctor gave him a prescription and told him he would get well. He picked up the prescription, went home, took the medicine, went to bed, and died. The only thing that the doctor and the pill changed was the way the man thought and felt when he died.

It did not make him well; it just made him feel better about his illness when he died. It gave him false hope. I have a fear this is exactly what happens to too many people, who say certain words and/or go through certain religious rituals. It changes the way they think and feel, but it does not change a thing about their spiritual life. They are still sinners.

Whatever words you want to use to tell God you are sorry for your sins and you want Him to forgive you, will work, if it is coming from your heart and not just your mouth. As my friend Robin, said, *"It is a heart issue, not a word issue."*

There may be many counterfeit conversions, which means there are many who are Christian in name only. They have never been born again, but they think they have. It is like the older gentleman that said he was a Christian in talk but not in walk.

A change is in the making

Read what Practical Word Studies in The New Testament says it means to repent.

To repent; to turn from one's sins; to change; to turn; to change one's mind; to turn one's life around.

In this Scripture, repentance is a turning away from sin and turning toward God. It is a change of mind, a forsaking of sin. It is putting sin out of one's thoughts and behavior. It is resolving never to think or do a thing again. (Cp. Matthew 3:2; Luke 13:2-3; Acts 2:38; Acts 3:19; Acts 8:22; Acts 26:20.) The change is turning away from lying, stealing, cheating, immorality, cursing, drunkenness, and the other so called glaring sins of the flesh. But the change is also turning away from the silent sins of the spirit such as self-centeredness, selfishness, envy, bitterness, pride, covetousness, anger, evil thoughts, hopelessness, laziness, jealousy, lust.

Repentance involves two turns. There is a negative turn away from sin and a positive turn toward God. It is a turning to God away from sin, whether sins of thought or action. (See POSB note, Repentance – § Luke 3:3. Cp. 1 Thes. 1:9; Acts 14:15.)

Repentance is more than sorrow. Sorrow may or may not be involved in repentance. A person may repent simply because he wills and acts to change; or a person may repent because he senses an agonizing sorrow within. But the sense or feeling of sorrow is not repentance. Repentance is both the change of mind and the actual turning of one's life away from sin and toward God. (See POSB Deeper Study #1 – § 2 Cor. 7:10.)

You **WILL NOT** have a transformed mind and you **ARE NOT** a new and different person, just because you go through some religious rituals, attend church, or you grew up in a Christian family and/or live in a Christian nation.

You **WILL** have a transformed mind... you **WILL** be a new and different person in the way you think and act... if you have really repented.

Repentance, turning your life over to God, does not mean you will not be tempted, but down deep inside – in your heart – the new you will not want to do the things the old you used to do. You will still be tempted, and may fall once-in-a-while, but you will get up, seek forgiveness, and move on into new territory of learning the ways of God and following them. Repentance is a defining point in your life; it redirects all that you are or ever want to be.

BECOMING A NEW AND DIFFERENT PERSON ON THE OUTSIDE BEGINS WITH BECOMING A NEW AND DIFFERENT PERSON ON THE INSIDE THAT CAN ONLY COME WITH REPENTANCE.

Years ago, I read a book titled *"INSIDE OUT"*, by Dr. Larry Crabb. I will give you a summary of the book with one sentence. We can only become the person God wants us to be when we start on the inside, the heart and the mind have to change.

Romans 12 says that we are to present ourselves to God in a way that is acceptable and pleasing to Him, then we will have a change in the way we think and feel about life and the way we live.

My friend, Daryl Worley, said this about repentance.

"I am afraid we have lost the definition of repentance. If you truly repent, you will be convicted to change the way you live your life. The total change may not be immediate but the conviction should be. Also, you will not ignore this conviction."

When you are born again, you will not want to live as you did before you came to Christ. You may be tempted, but you will not want to follow the patterns you followed before you repented and turned to Christ because you are a new person in your thinking and living.

Romans 12:1-2 (TLB) "And so, dear brothers, I plead with you to give your bodies to God. Let them be a living sacrifice, holy – the kind he can accept. When you think of what he has done for you, is this too much to ask? Do not copy the behavior and customs of this world, but be a new and different person with a fresh newness in all you do and think."

Romans 12:2 (NIV) "Do not conform any longer to the pattern of this world, but be transformed by the renewing of your mind. Then you will be able to test and approve what God's will is--his good, pleasing and perfect will."

Notice in the (NIV) it says, *"...be transformed by the renewing of your mind"*. Renewing is a process. Some people claim that God changed them totally and instantly when they repented. I do not say it did not happen to them, but it did not happen to me.

This scripture is telling us that if we say we are Christians we should live like Christians. Those are great instructions, but when we have been doing something a long time, it is hard to change. This scripture not only tells what we are to do, it tells us how. Change the way you think by renewing your mind. This starts with a change in the heart – the spirit – the part of us that connects with God.

➢ *How do we break the bad patterns we have been following?*

➢ *How do we change our questionable behavior?*

➢ *How do we change the way we think?*

➢ *How do we keep from following after the ways of the world?*

➢ *How do we escape the traps of Satan?*

We repent and turn our lives over to God. He sends His Holy Spirit to assist us in living a new life. We have a power in us that we have never had before. We read and study the Bible consistently and allow it to begin to transform and renew our minds.

- If you have truly repented, you will become a new and different person via your transformed mind.
- The transformed mind will help you break the bad patterns you have been following.
- The transformed mind will help you change your bad behavior.
- The transformed mind will help keep you from following after the ways of the world because you will think differently.

- The Holy Spirit via the transformed mind will show you a way to free yourself from the traps of Satan.
- The Holy Spirit will give you **will power** that you never had before.

John 14:16-17 (TLB) [16] *and I will ask the Father and he will give you another Comforter, and he will never leave you.* [17] *He is the Holy Spirit, the Spirit who leads into all truth. The world at large cannot receive him, for it isn't looking for him and doesn't recognize him. But you do, for he lives with you now and some day shall be in you.*

I am going to take you on a walk through what, in my opinion, may be the most important chapter in the Bible for new Christians. I am going to give you the last verse now, then come back to it later. This verse sums it all up. Yes, you get it one more time. I hope this becomes embedded in your mind.

Romans 12:21 Do not be overcome by evil, but overcome evil with good.

Before you became a Christian, your evil nature controlled you, now that you are a Christian, you have the spirit of God helping you control yourself. The following should describe your life. If it does not, there is something wrong.

Galatians 5:22-26 (TLB) 22 BUT WHEN THE HOLY SPIRIT CONTROLS OUR LIVES he will produce this kind of fruit in us: love, joy, peace, patience, kindness, goodness, faithfulness, 23 gentleness and self-control; and here there is no conflict with Jewish laws.
24 Those who belong to Christ have nailed their natural evil desires to his cross and crucified them there.
25 If we are living now by the Holy Spirit's power, let us follow the Holy Spirit's leading in every part of our lives.

You can live a clean righteous life with the Holy Spirit's power and you can overcome evil by doing the good the scripture tells us to do. You have to choose on purpose to do it.

> *Yes, I know, here I go again, it is repeat, repeat, repeat, that is the way you lock something into your mind. Say it three times right now.*

Romans 12:21 Do not be overcome by evil, but overcome evil with good.

Your best defense is a good offense. Charge, move forward doing the good you know you are to do. Be so busy doing good that your mind and your actions are preoccupied with the good you are doing.

Let us be honest. The pull of the world is very strong and overwhelming and sometimes very appealing to the imperfectible mind and flesh. The Bible says we are in a spiritual war, the pull of darkness – unrighteousness, vs. the pull of the light – righteousness.

It is the good against the bad. Do not be deceived; it is a real battle – a spiritual battle. Unless we repent and follow Christ and allow the Holy Spirit of God to have control in our lives, the pull of sin and unrighteousness <u>**will always**</u> overcome us. No matter how hard we may try, we will lose in the end.

We cannot overpower Satan and sin – the trapper and his traps – by ourselves. We cannot be acceptable to God as sinners. Our only hope is to repent – be born again – start anew – give up the old life – take on a new life. Present yourself to God and say, "Here I am; I am committed to following you and doing what you want me to do". Then you go and do good to and for others. Doing good does not make you righteous, righteousness makes you do good.

We are going to look at Romans 12 again and this time we are going to personalize it. The next 18 verses of Romans 12 tell us what we are to do, how we are to live, after we present ourselves to God. These are the good things we will be doing, that will keep us busy.

As a Christian, you are part of the family of God. You are brothers and sisters in Christ. In some ways, this spiritual bond is greater than the bond with our blood siblings. You can be physical siblings, and have different thoughts, desires, dreams, plans, and drives and go in different ways with different endings. As spiritual siblings, we have a common goal and a destination that is the same.

> *Romans 12:4-5 (TLB) "Just as there are many parts to our bodies, so it is with Christ's body. ₅ We are all parts of it, and it takes every one of us to make it complete, for we each have different work to do. So we belong to each other, and each needs all the others."*

When you repented, you became part of God's family. God has given you some kind of a blessing – gift –talent – ability to do good. It is your responsibility to use it in a way that is beneficial to others. Do not say you cannot do anything or you do not have any abilities. If you are one of God's children, God gave you some ability to do something good to and for others. This scripture says God has given all of us some kind of gift to benefit others.

➢ *As you work your way through this list of gifts, abilities, talents, make a check in your mind (or even underline) the abilities that may fit you. You may not be proficient with this gift yet, but God will help you develop this ability as you use it. You and the one you are doing good to or for will receive blessings.*

Romans 12:6-8 (TLB)
⁶ God has given each of us the ability to do certain things well.

So if God has given you the ability to prophesy, then prophesy whenever you can – as often as your faith is strong enough to receive a message from God.
7 If your gift is that of serving others, serve them well. If you are a teacher, do a good job of teaching.
8 If you are a preacher, see to it that your sermons are strong and helpful. If God has given you money, be generous in helping others with it. If God has given you administrative ability and put you in charge of the work of others, take the responsibility seriously. Those who offer comfort to the sorrowing should do so with Christian cheer.

We need to take seriously the work that God wants us to do. Do not do just enough to get by. Give it your best shot. Do not be lazy or indifferent – "serve well" – "do a good job of teaching" – "strong and helpful". Take your responsibility seriously.

Make what you do for God, the number one issue in your life. Get your "**P**riorities" right. The other things you do will come second to doing what God wants you to do for Him. Do what He wants you to do with enthusiasm and excitement. If you do, you will enjoy doing it more than you will if you whine about having to do it.

Have you noticed whiners are generally unhappy people? It is a "**P**riority" and/or "**A**ttitude" problem.

I have found it to be fun, exciting, and rewarding to look for ways to be helpful to others. I do not say this boastfully, I say it as a testimony. Sometimes I have driven hundreds of miles, spent a night or two in a motel and bought my own meals to do something special, something good for someone else.

I have worked with my hands all day long helping friends with personal needs.

I have spent many retirement days helping others with work projects on their home.

Sometimes I have given up an evening I had planned so I could listen for an hour or two, to problems, hurts, frustrations and troubles, pray with someone and encourage them.

Now that I am retired, I have found doing the same things I did when I was pastoring and being paid for it, is much more rewarding now with no pay.

I am finding out in a new and different way, *"How His ways really satisfy"*. (Romans 12:2 TLB) I actually feel better about what I am doing without pay than I felt when I was being paid.

Doing good to and for others does not have to be something big. It can be as simple as picking up your phone and calling someone and saying, *"I was just thinking about you and wanted to tell you how much I appreciate your involvement in the music program. The music Sunday was awesome."*

Teaching is not just a profession with a classroom of people. It is a responsibility to God to represent Him well in what you teach others by word and/or example.

The other day we were walking at the mall. I saw this young daddy bent down, looking his probably 4-year-old daughter right in the eyes and very gently talking to her as mother stood silently by. I could tell that this was a teaching moment.

When he finished I motioned to him that I would like to talk to him. I told him I had observed what he was doing and complimented him for seizing the moment to do some teaching and doing it with gentleness, kindness and love.

He did a good thing, and I did a good thing when I blessed him with a compliment. I gave him encouragement to continue being a good daddy. I confirmed what he was doing, and I encouraged him to keep doing it.

Everybody needs confirmation when doing good things. My word processing program keeps telling me to use "well" where I am using good. Ok, Mr. Microsoft Word, check this out.

What we are doing, we should do well.

I am talking about:

- Doing good
- Living right
- Honoring God in the way we live
- Helping others
- Loving others
- Forgiving others
- Seeking forgiveness
- Feeding the hungry
- Meeting needs
- Showing compassion
- And more

You know what I am talking about, don't you?

We can serve and share in a spirit of love and obedience to God or we can do it grudgingly and with a bad spirit. The bad spirit could be an indication that our *Priority* may be right, but our *Attitude* needs to be worked on. We know what the right thing to do is, but our attitude toward doing it is rotten.

Romans 12:6-8 (TLB) tells us we are to help, show, instruct, comfort, and encourage others and do it with a cheerful *Attitude*. Do not grumble; be cheerful concerning the things you feel God wants you to do. Remember the title of this sub-point is, **"This is what you do"**.

➤ *Put an "S" for strength or a "W" for weakness where it applies to you.*

8 If God has given you money, be generous in helping others with it.

If God has given you administrative ability and put you in charge of the work of others, take the responsibility seriously.

Those who offer comfort to the sorrowing should do so with Christian cheer.

9 Do not just pretend that you love others: really love them.
Hate what is wrong.
Stand on the side of the good.

Christians may be too passive at times in the name of kindness. There may be times when we need to speak up and take a stand on the side of righteousness with a good spirit lest it appear that we are condoning the wrong.

My definition of love is, "Love is caring enough to challenge someone, even hurt them if necessary, in order to help them."

LOVE IS CARING ENOUGH TO CHALLENGE SOMEONE - EVEN HURT THEM IF NECESSARY, IN ORDER TO HELP THEM.

You do not always make others feel good when you are trying to help them. I believe we have a responsibility to challenge people at times concerning the way they are living. When the challenge is done the right way, with the right spirit, at the right time, it is an act of love.

A few weeks ago, a man that was in the youth department in the church I pastored many years ago did a really stupid and sinful thing. It would have been considered a "big sin" with some severe consequences. He contacted me and told me about his circumstances, and asked for help. I asked him if I could send him some material that I think could help him. He said I could.

I was very kind, but very firm and straight about my disappointment with his actions, and I sent him the chapter that I had just finished, "*__The Starting Point__*". He responded and thanked me. He told me he really regretted what he had done and that he was very sorry. He assured me he would work through the material I had sent him and that he appreciated what I said to him and signed the e-mail "love you".

WOW! I was overcome with the way he responded to my challenge to him that he needed to repent, seek forgiveness from those he had wronged and change the way he was living.

It would have been very easy for him to get defensive because my speaking about his sinful act and my challenge were both strong, and with love. I was not even sure he would reply. He knew me, he knew I loved him and cared about him because of the love I gave him when I was his pastor.

I have many times said to someone in a counseling session something like this. "You have to come to me for help. Do you think I, as your pastor, love you and care about you? Do you think I really want to help you? Do you think I want the best for you?" I required them to answer each question. After they answered, I would continue with a statement similar to this. "Sometimes the best for us is not what we want, but it is what we need. Do you want me to give you what I think you need, or do you want me to make you feel good?"

I think real love, genuine love, requires us to challenge each other at times. This is a difficult thing to do because we do not want to hurt anyone. We do not like to run the risk of confrontation. We want peace, so we do not do what we really should do or say what we really should say because we want to avoid any kind of conflict.

Continuing on in Romans 12 (TLB)

➤ *Put an "S" for strength or a "W" for weakness where it applies to you.*

10 Love each other with brotherly affection and take delight in honoring each other.

11 Never be lazy in your work, but serve the Lord enthusiastically.

➤ *Is there someone you have a hard time loving and honoring? If so, why?*

➤ *What can you do to resolve that?*

➤ *How enthusiastic are you about serving the Lord in all things, even those things you do not want to do?*

There may be times we have to force ourselves to do what we know we should do. We do it because it is high on our <u>Priority</u> list – it is what God wants us to do. There will be times when we will not feel any enthusiasm, any excitement, any interest, or any passion for doing what we know we should do. We will have to work on our <u>Attitude</u> – the way we are thinking and feeling about it. Remember our mind and our feelings cannot be perfected, so we just have to <u>Discipline</u> ourselves.

➤ *Do you catch yourself making excuses and rationalizing when you know you should do a certain thing but don't want to? How has that worked for you? Has it fixed the problem? Has it made you a better person? Has it resolved any differences between you and someone else? Has it given you more peace?*

Do not make excuses and rationalize. Just do it and the enthusiasm will begin to build as you obediently follow the will of God for your life. Then you can actually enjoy what you are doing because it is the right thing to do. The bonus will be an improvement in your *Attitude.*

Some caution here. There are some, who have a tendency to overdo and burn out. They often become bitter and cynical. This can actually be a trap of Satan. If Satan fails to get you to be disobedient and do nothing, then he will try to get you to overdo and become cynical and develop an *Attitude* that hinders rather than helps.

Here are more clear instructions from Romans 12 (TLB) on how you are to present yourself to God in a pleasing and acceptable way.

➢ *Try to identify those things that you are weak in or strong in. Put a "S" for strength or a "W" for weakness where it applies to you.*

12 Be glad for all God is planning for you. Be patient in trouble, and prayerful always.

13 When God's children are in need, you be the one to help them out. And get into the habit of inviting guests home for dinner or, if they need lodging, for the night.

14 If someone mistreats you because you are a Christian, do not curse him; pray that God will bless him.

15 When others are happy, be happy with them. If they are sad, share their sorrow.

16 Work happily together. Do not try to act big. Do not try to get into the good graces of important people, but enjoy the company of ordinary folks. And do not think you know it all!

17 Never pay back evil for evil. Do things in such a way that everyone can see you are honest clear through.

18 Do not quarrel with anyone. Be at peace with everyone, just as much as possible.

NIV 18 If it is possible, as far as it depends on you, live at peace with everyone.

19 Dear friends, never avenge yourselves. Leave that to God, for he has said that he will repay those who deserve it. [Do not take the law into your own hands.]

20 Instead, feed your enemy if he is hungry. If he is thirsty give him something to drink and you will be "heaping coals of fire on his head." In other words, he will feel ashamed of himself for what he has done to you.

This next one is big, powerful, and commanding. It sums it all up.

21 Do not be overcome by evil, but overcome evil with good.

Spend as much of your time as you can, looking for opportunities to do as much good as you can, to as many people as you can. Focus on as many ways as you can to do good to everyone everywhere!

Romans 12:2(TLB): Do not copy the behavior and customs of this world, but be a new and different person with a fresh newness in all you do and think. Then you will learn from your own experience how his ways will really satisfy you.

Jesus said, *"I have come that you may have life to the full."* I think that means He wants us to have a really good, great, awesome life. He wants us to be fulfilled, happy, contented, satisfied. He wants us to like who and what we are.

HE WANTS US TO MOVE
"OUT OF THE DARKNESS INTO THE LIGHT."

The Christian life is about finding true satisfaction, feeling truly fulfilled and complete, liking who and what we are. God wants us to have a wonderful life, but this wonderful life has to start with a right relationship with Him. We have to do it His way, not the ways of the world.

This is what you do:

- Repent and be born again.
- Present yourself to God in an acceptable way.
- Quit following the sinful ways of the world.
- Renew – rebuild the mind – the way you think.
- Live the life of a new person in Christ.

Caution!

Good works alone will not do it. Many good people do good things. Their nature is just good. Almost everything they do is good. Their **P**riorities are good. Their **A**ttitude is good. Becoming a Christian will not change much in the way they live. They just lack one thing. Their heart is still dark. They are born sinners. They are good sinners, but they are still sinners.

Romans 3:23 (TLB) "Yes, all have sinned; all fall short of God's glorious ideal…"

1 John 1:8-10 (TLB) 8 If we say that we have no sin, we are only fooling ourselves and refusing to accept the truth.
9 But if we confess our sins to him, he can be depended on to

forgive us and to cleanse us from every wrong. [And it is perfectly proper for God to do this for us because Christ died to wash away our sins.]

10 If we claim we have not sinned, we are lying and calling God a liar, for he says we have sinned.

If you lack understanding at this point, go back to the chapter, "The Starting Point" and read it again. We are all born sinners and need to come to the place where we understand that and confess our belief in Jesus Christ as our Savior and ask Him to forgive the sins we have committed and then quit sinning and start following His teachings.

This is what you get

The good life here on this planet

I am talking about true, long lasting satisfaction, not something that gives you initial gratification for a while then sends you on a trip to find more "make me feel good" food.

John 14:27 (TLB) [27] *"I am leaving you with a gift – peace of mind and heart! And the peace I give isn't fragile like the peace the world gives. So don't be troubled or afraid.*

Romans 12:2: " (TLB) ... Then you will learn from your own experience how his ways will really SATISFY you.

When we are truly serving God, we get to experience real, true, lasting ***SATISFACTION***. We will have inner peace, fulfillment, happiness, and contentment that the things of the world cannot give. That is what we are all seeking. That is what we really want. That is what we give our time, effort, energy, and money for –***SATISFACTION and PEACE***.

When you use what God has given you, to bless, benefit, and help others, you will be blessed. You will find a true satisfaction that can only be found in serving God.

Following the instructions in Romans 12 on how to live, calls for a personal sacrifice just as the Bible said it would. It also leads to true satisfaction in life that can only come by doing what God wants us to do. We do those things that our renewed, transformed mind tells us to do and as a result, we will find true satisfaction in living. There will still be some bumps, maybe even tragedies in life, but in some miraculous way, we still have a deep settled peace that the world can't explain.

- To be satisfied means to be contented.
- To be satisfied is to be pleased with who and what we are.
- To be satisfied is to feel complete and fulfilled.

If we have not repented and turned to Christ, the "old man" with the sinful nature, will rule. The old mind in the "old man" will tell us lies to get us to follow the ways and the patterns of the world. We will do things we hate ourselves for doing. The old sinful mind tells us that the things of the world will satisfy us, so we do those things, and we are still not satisfied. We still lack what we are really wanting. We do what we do because we believe what we are doing will bring satisfaction.

If we have repented and turned to Christ, we will have a renewed, transformed mind that will give us instructions that will provide true lasting satisfaction. This changed mind will not happen overnight – the changed heart will; then as we read, study and pray, the mind will become like the mind of Christ.

God wants us to have a wonderful life. That is His goal for us. However, we have to do it His way if we are going to find that satisfaction and fulfillment in life that He wants us to have.

When our transformed mind finally understands that, we will find real satisfaction – what we are looking for – by doing the things that God wants us to do, we will begin to make changes in what we do. Our _Priorities_ will change. Our _Attitude_ will change. We will start doing things differently.

This is the payoff, the reward and the incentive. Contentment, satisfaction, happiness, and the good life will come... when we present ourselves to God in a holy and acceptable way.

➤ *Do you want the good life here on this earth?*

➤ *Are you willing to do what you know you have to do to get it?*

The perfect life in heaven

The good life here on this earth is still going to have some imperfections, some struggles, some disappointments, and frustrations. It is going to be far better than it was before we repented and started following Christ, but we are still going to face natural consequences of a fallen race. Eventually, we get heaven, if we don't get discouraged and give up. Heaven should be our first _P_riority and the final goal.

John 3:16-17 (NIV) "For God so loved the world that he gave his one and only Son, that whoever believes in him shall not perish

BUT HAVE ETERNAL LIFE.17 For God did not send his Son into the world to condemn the world, but to save the world through him."

Revelation 21:1-27 (NLT)
[1] Then I saw a new heaven and a new earth, for the old heaven and the old earth had disappeared. And the sea was also gone.
[2] And I saw the holy city, the new Jerusalem, coming down from God out of heaven like a bride beautifully dressed for her husband.
[3] I heard a loud shout from the throne, saying, "Look, God's home is now among his people! He will live with them, and they will be his people. God himself will be with them.
[4] He will wipe every tear from their eyes, and there will be no more death or sorrow or crying or pain. All these things are gone forever."
[5] And the one sitting on the throne said, "Look, I am making everything new!" And then he said to me, "Write this down, for what I tell you is trustworthy and true."
[6] And he also said, "It is finished! I am the Alpha and the Omega — the Beginning and the End. To all who are thirsty I will give freely from the springs of the water of life.
[7] All who are victorious will inherit all these blessings, and I will be their God, and they will be my children.
[8] "But cowards, unbelievers, the corrupt, murderers, the immoral, those who practice witchcraft, idol worshipers, and all liars — their fate is in the fiery lake of burning sulfur. This is the second death."
[9] Then one of the seven angels who held the seven bowls containing the seven last plagues came and said to me, "Come with me! I will show you the bride, the wife of the Lamb."
[10] So he took me in the Spirit to a great, high mountain, and he showed me the holy city, Jerusalem, descending out of heaven from God.
[11] It shone with the glory of God and sparkled like a precious stone — like jasper as clear as crystal.

¹² *The city wall was broad and high, with twelve gates guarded by twelve angels. And the names of the twelve tribes of Israel were written on the gates.*

¹³ *There were three gates on each side — east, north, south, and west.*

¹⁴ *The wall of the city had twelve foundation stones, and on them were written the names of the twelve apostles of the Lamb.*

¹⁵ *The angel who talked to me held in his hand a gold measuring stick to measure the city, its gates, and its wall.*

¹⁶ *When he measured it, he found it was a square, as wide as it was long. In fact, its length and width and height were each 1,400 miles.*

¹⁷ *Then he measured the walls and found them to be 216 feet thick (according to the human standard used by the angel).*

¹⁸ *The wall was made of jasper, and the city was pure gold, as clear as glass.*

¹⁹ *The wall of the city was built on foundation stones inlaid with twelve precious stones: the first was jasper, the second sapphire, the third agate, the fourth emerald,*

²⁰ *the fifth onyx, the sixth carnelian, the seventh chrysolite, the eighth beryl, the ninth topaz, the tenth chrysoprase, the eleventh jacinth, the twelfth amethyst.*

²¹ *The twelve gates were made of pearls — each gate from a single pearl! And the main street was pure gold, as clear as glass.*

²² *I saw no temple in the city, for the Lord God Almighty and the Lamb are its temple.*

²³ *And the city has no need of sun or moon, for the glory of God illuminates the city, and the Lamb is its light.*

²⁴ *The nations will walk in its light, and the kings of the world will enter the city in all their glory.*

²⁵ *Its gates will never be closed at the end of day because there is no night there.*

²⁶ *And all the nations will bring their glory and honor into the city.*

²⁷ *Nothing evil will be allowed to enter, nor anyone who practices*

shameful idolatry and dishonesty – but only those whose names are written in the Lamb's Book of Life.

This is what you do

- Repent and be born again.
- Present yourself to God in an acceptable way.
- Quit following the sinful ways of the world.
- Renew – rebuild the mind, the way you think.
- Live the life of a new person in Christ.

This is what you get

- True satisfaction – the good life – on this earth
- Eternal life in heaven with God forever

This is how you do it

Live by **the "PADD"** **P**riorities, **A**ttitude, **D**iscipline, **D**etermination.

Priorities

You get your **Priorities** straight. After you repent, find out what God thinks and feels about things. Find out what God says is important and make that important to you. Make pleasing God your most important priority. Make it your ultimate priority because that would include going to heaven. Follow His lead in placing values on things, people, and actions.

Why I wrote these books!

After retirement, I just wanted to be foot-loose and fancy-free. I was. I enjoyed it. I did n ot want any regular responsibilities. I filled the pulpit now and then for vacationing pastors. I did a couple of short interims and a few other little ministry things, but about 95% of my time was free.

One day about 3 years ago, I had this feeling that I was wasting my time. There was something inside me saying, "You need to be doing something worthwhile with your time."

I replied, "Ok Lord, if this is you, give me some direction." I began to feel a strong urge to write a book. I struggled with a title to cover my three main concerns. (1) People's individual salvation, unsaved people and deceived people – people who think they are Christ-followers, but they are not. (2) The Church's role in America. (3) The need for America to refocus and become a nation "UNDER GOD" again.

I settled for **OUT OF THE DARKNESS, INTO THE LIGHT.** That seemed like a title that could include all three of the areas. Because it was so large, I decided to split it into two books.

The first book is **CHOOSING HEAVEN – A Soul Searching Adventure.** (138 pages) This book is about you and me as individuals – our personal lives. This has to do with our individual choices and responsibilities. We can become better people and experience better lives through Christ living in us. This book is about you and me becoming winners now (this world) and forever (heaven). It covers repentance and the changed life, the old you vs. the new you. This book is based on these scriptures.

John 3:3(TLB): Jesus said, "With all the earnestness I possess I tell you this: Unless you are born again, you can never get into the Kingdom of God."

Romans 12: 1 Therefore, I urge you, brothers, in view of God's mercy, to offer your bodies as living sacrifices, holy and pleasing to God–this is your spiritual act of worship. 2 Do not conform any longer to the pattern of this world, but be transformed by the renewing of your mind. Then you will be able to test and approve what God's will is–his good, pleasing and perfect will. (NIV)

The second book is **SAVING AMERICA –Starting With The Church.** (154 pages) This is about you and me with individual responsibilities becoming part of a group, the church – the body of Christ, whose combined responsibility is to make life better for all. If you or I fail as an individual, the whole body is injured, thus hindering the work God wants and expects in and from His church.

Our only hope for **SAVING AMERICA** is the church, Christ-followers. If there is conflict/division among the individuals in the church, the church as a whole is less effective in all it stands for and all it does. That means we have to stay spiritually healthy and effective in **SAVING AMERICA.**

If someone in the church is not carrying their share of the load – doing the work God wants them to do, the work of the church is hindered. It is vital that each individual Christ-follower understand what God expects from them. It is equally important that each individual follower of Christ, does what God wants them to do.

This book is about the church **SAVING AMERICA** and helping us all be winners. I say it again. Our only hope for **SAVING AMERICA** is the church – true Christ-followers. The Politicians have tried over and over and have always and will continue to fail. We have a spiritual problem in America, that can only be fixed as those who claim to be followers of Christ become true followers of Christ.

I see this book as a great small group study. It will cause every professing Christian to re-examine their relationship with God. *Ephesians 4:16 (TLB) 16 Under his direction, the whole body is fitted together perfectly, and each part in its own special way helps the other parts, so that the whole body is healthy and growing and full of love.*

Order **CHOOSING HEAVEN** (138 pages) or **SAVING AMERICA – Starting With The Church** (154 pages) from Amazon for $6.99 paperback + tax & shipping, about $11. Order through me in quantity for less than $4.00 a book, depending on the number, tax, & shipping. Kindle version is $0.99. Order a paperback from Amazon and get the Kindle version free. These books make great personal devotional books to help you take a close look at your personal spiritual life and help you in some of the areas where you struggle. They are also good gift books and great small group study books.

N. Rene Colaw, Nrlaw@cableone.net, 2621 Rabbit Ridge Road Bartlesville, Ok – 74006, 913-333-1966

Attitude

You develop a winning, God-like **Attitude** – a new and better attitude. You start thinking and feeling like God thinks and feels about things. Your God-like attitude – your transformed mind will direct everything you do and say toward Godly living – righteousness. This transformed mind redirects the way you think and feel about everything, which will change what you do and do not do.

Discipline

You begin to **Discipline** yourself. You make yourself do what you know is right just because it is right. Do what you know and know what you do… IS RIGHT!

Determination

You become very **Determined** – strong minded, single minded, and unwavering in your drive to live the way God wants you to live. Nothing is going to get in the way of your loving and serving God.

Romans 12:1(TLB) "And so, dear brothers, I plead with you to give your bodies to God. Let them BE A LIVING SACRIFICE, HOLY – the kind he can accept. When you think of what he has done for you, is this too much to ask?"

➢ **Which of these four things do you need to work on the most: (1) get your Priorities straight, (2) develop a new and better Attitude, (3) begin to Discipline yourself, (4) become very Determined to do what you know is right?**

➢ **Who are you going to ask to help you, make you accountable, hold you responsible?**

FIVE

IT'S ALL ABOUT YOU

- ➤ *Where do you stand spiritually today – right now?*

- ➤ *Have you accepted His gift of eternal life?*

- ➤ *Have you repented?*

- ➤ *Are you born again?*

- ➤ *Are you going to heaven? Are you sure – or do you just think you are?*

Answer these questions with a yes or no.

THIS BOOK HAS *CONFIRMED* MY BELIEF THAT I AM A CHRISTIAN AND HEADED TO HEAVEN.

_____ I have felt true sorrow for (I regret) my sins and have told God I was sorry that I had been living a life that was sinful and offensive to Him.

_____ I have confessed my belief in Jesus Christ as my only hope of salvation and sought forgiveness for my sins

_____ I have told God that I am committed to turning my life around, quit living as I had been, and live for Christ by following His teachings.

_____ I know without a doubt that my sins are forgiven and I am ready to go to heaven.

THIS BOOK HAS *CONFRONTED* ME ABOUT MY SINS AND I AM *CONCERNED* ABOUT MY FUTURE.

_____I have been confronted. I have known for a long time that I need to do something about the way I am living. I know I need to make things right between me and God. I am not ready for Heaven.

_____Until I read this book I had not felt any sorrow (regret) for my sins, but I do feel that kind of sorrow (regret) right now. I never realized before how offensive I had been to God. I am really sorry.

_____I do believe in Jesus Christ, and I believe He is my only hope of salvation. I do want His forgiveness for my sins. I am asking Him right now to forgive me and come into my life

_____I really do want to turn my life around and live so God is pleased with me. I want to do the things He wants me to do and live the way He wants me to live.

_____I will do whatever I can to grow in my faith and learn more about God's ways. This will include personal Bible reading and study, involvement in a group Bible study, and attending a Bible teaching church where I can become involved.

I DO NOT FIT IN EITHER OF THE ABOVE. THIS IS WHERE I AM.

_____I do not feel any pull toward God but I want to. I would like the Holy Spirit of God to move in my life – knock on my spiritual door – and draw me to Him. I have learned a lot from this book and I want to know that I am going to be able to go to heaven.

_____I have not done anything about my salvation, and I do not feel a need to do anything. I still do not have any concern about going to heaven.

If you still do not understand repentance and salvation go back and reread the chapter, The Starting Point. Ask God to open your mind and your heart to what He wants you to hear.

BIBLIOGRAPHY

- Butler, Trent C., ed. *Holman Bible Dictionary*. Nashville, TN: Holman Bible Publishers, 1991. WORD*search* CROSS e-book.
- *Life Application Study Bible*. Wheaton, IL: Tyndale, 1988. WORD*search* CROSS e-book.
- *The Holy Bible: New International Version* Grand Rapids: Zondervan, 1984. WORD*search* CROSS e-book.
- *The Holy Bible: New King James Version* Nashville: Thomas Nelson, 1988. WORD*search* CROSS e-book.
- *Holy Bible, New Living Translation* Wheaton, IL: Tyndale House Publishers, 2004. WORD*search* CROSS e-book.
- Peterson, Eugene H., ed. – *The Message: The Bible in Contemporary Language* Colorado Springs, CO: NavPress, 2002. WORD*search* CROSS e-book.
- *Practical Word Studies in The New Testament*. Chattanooga: Leadership Ministries Worldwide, 1998. WORD*search* CROSS e-book.
- "Take my Life and Let it be" Francis Havergal, 1836 – 1879